Marketing Today's Academic Library

A Bold New Approach to Communicating with Students

BRIAN MATHEWS

AMERICAN LIBRARY ASSOCIATION

Chicago 2009

Brian Mathews is the user experience librarian at the Georgia Institute of Technology. He has an MLIS from the University of South Florida. He has published numerous journal articles and is an active speaker and panel member on a variety of library topics, particularly on increasing the awareness of library services to students. His blog is *The Ubiquitous Librarian:* http://theubiquitouslibrarian.typepad.com.

The paper used in this publication meets the minimum requirements of American National Standard for Information Sciences—Permanence of Paper for Printed Library Materials, ANSI Z39.48-1992. ∞

Library of Congress Cataloging-in-Publication Data

Mathews, Brian (Brian Scott)

Marketing today's academic library : a bold new approach to communicating with students / Brian Mathews.

p. cm.

Includes bibliographical references and index.

ISBN 978-0-8389-0984-3 (alk. paper)

1. Academic libraries—Marketing. 2. Academic libraries—Public relations. 3. Libraries and students. 4. Advertising—Libraries. I. Title.

Z716.3.M344 2009

021.7—dc22 2008047408

ISBN-13: 978-0-8389-0984-3

Printed in the United States of America

13 12 11 10 09 5 4 3 2 1

Dedicated to college students around the world, who deserve better library experiences

Contents

Foreword

MOST LIBRARIANS DID NOT ENTER THIS profession because of a passion for marketing. Despite this, marketing skills have become a key element of a successful career in the field. At the same time, marketing itself has become far more complicated—it is no longer merely enough to craft a good message. To be successful today, a relevant marketer must also master the media through which his message is conveyed. In other words, this transformation of the role of librarian has happened during a time when it has never been more difficult to become an effective marketer.

This challenge is not unique to your profession. In my field—e-commerce and distribution channel management—it took me about twelve years to admit that I was a marketer. My professional life has been focused on consumer-facing Internet (and other emerging media) business models since 1995, and my four patents all concern performance-based business models that are enabled by these media. Even so, for a long time I thought of myself as a general business manager who liked technology. Three years ago, I was rewarded for my e-commerce success by being given responsibility for the other distribution channels used by my company, InterContinental Hotels Group, in the Americas region. The name of our department was to become Distribution Marketing, a decidedly unsexy label that seemed to lack the geek-chic of my prior roles. However, after briefly considering a protest, I was finally forced to recognize that, as someone who spent all of his working life figuring out ways to influence consumer behavior, I was, in fact, a marketer and would just have to deal with it.

The thing is, marketing is *hard.* It always has been, but in the past decade and a half it has gotten a whole lot harder. In the pre-Internet days, marketers had to worry about

1. Who they needed to target their offerings to
2. Where those people could be reached
3. What message to send them

In addition, they had a theoretical obligation to track the results of their efforts. This was often very difficult or even impossible to do and was often left out for the sake of expediency, giving rise to a common measurement philosophy: "Half of my advertising budget is wasted, I just don't know which half!" The good news was that there were really only a handful of media available to choose from (challenge number two)—outdoor advertising, print, and broadcast, with a pretty significant concentration of audiences within each medium.

As you will learn in this remarkable book for librarians, today's marketers have all of these traditional challenges compounded by a much wider array of media choices (expanding daily), far less audience concentration, and a target consumer base that is increasingly empowered to control their exposure to marketing messages based on their individual definitions of relevance, intrusiveness, style, and convenience. Perversely, we have also entered the Age of Marketing Accountability, spurred by the exacting precision by which the actual value of online marketing can be measured, so the old adage about measurement futility has now been banished from the workplace as a relic of the past. As I said, marketing is *hard.*

While there is no magic formula for marketing success (and if there were, I would probably keep the secret to myself), there have emerged a few clear-cut recipes for failure. One such doomed approach is to determinedly ignore new and emerging media while clinging to anything that worked in the past. Any librarian-marketer who has ambitions for repeated success *must* embrace an early adopter-tester philosophy combined with a willingness to tolerate failure on a regular basis. If the target audience includes the eighteen- to twenty-nine-year-old generation, this mandate is amplified at least fourfold.

As Brian Mathews will explain in practical terms, this means you, the marketer (it's OK, you can admit it), should start off each day thinking about how you might want to leverage some new communication medium. How will you leverage the iPhone? The chumby? Twitter?

Facebook and MySpace? Nintendo Wii and Microsoft Xbox? Have you updated your library website with the latest usability and functional conventions and expectations of your audience? Are you keeping up with the latest organic search indexing algorithms on Google? What about the wild world of wikis and Web 2.0? (As I write this, I think of someone picking up Brian's book in fifteen years, reading this foreword, and mistaking it for a user's guide to some kind of museum of antiquities. Will anyone even be reading then—or will Web 6.0/Mobile 12G include some way of beaming desired data right into the brain from the ether? Will we market directly to our audiences at all, or will the "market *through,* not *to*" model have emerged as the dominant means of influencing behavior and consumer choice?)

As librarians, you don't have to answer all these questions, but you do have to *try* to answer them. You also need to keep up with what everyone around you is trying to do in order to avoid repeating their mistakes. In other words, strap in and hold on—this is going to be a wild ride!

Brian's book is targeted to the unique marketing challenges within the media sciences world—particularly with respect to influencing the mercurial student market, but its message is relevant to any consumer marketer in the modern world. (The irony of media/archival specialists using a *book* to learn about the potential of new media is not lost on us—Gutenberg would be pleased to know that his invention has yet to be surpassed as a vehicle of knowledge-sharing!) I think you will enjoy it, but please take some time to *act* on it as well!

Del Ross
Vice President of Distribution
Marketing, InterContinental
Hotels Group

Acknowledgments

THE GEORGIA TECH LIBRARY WAS A FERtile testing ground for many of the ideas described in this book. Thanks to my colleagues for their support and encouragement. Thanks to Crit Stuart for our many conversations about challenging mainstream thinking on libraries and for teaching me to become holistic and customer-sensitive. Thanks to Steven Bell for all the reading recommendations and career advice. A *big* thank-you to Tara Patterson; without her careful eye this book would be filled with unnecessary commas and poor phrasing. Thanks to Dottie Hunt for graphics assistance with this and all our other projects. Thanks to ALA for taking a risk on the Ubiquitous Librarian. Thanks to my patient and loving hunsta wife Leslie. Thanks to my mom for taking me to libraries at a young age and always encouraging me to read. And finally, thanks to the hundreds of students who took the time to talk to me about their library experiences.

Prologue

Becoming Ubiquitous

TWENTY PAIRS OF EYES STARED AHEAD AS I demonstrated several library databases. The class had a paper due in a few weeks, so most of them were following along. I did notice, however, one student typing away on his PDA throughout the entire instructional session. He appeared to be texting or perhaps playing a game, but he was quiet and didn't bother the others, so I let it go. With fifteen minutes left before the end of the period, I let the students search for articles while I offered assistance. As I passed Mr. PDA I saw that he was searching Google. Long story short, he told me he didn't like using an "old school" computer and that he did all of his searching on his BlackBerry. Apparently he could not get through our proxy, so he was using the open Web instead. I made a note to talk with our systems department and then, instead of forcing him to use our "traditional" computers, I helped him the best I could via his phone.

The story could have ended there with a moral on customizing services to meet students' needs, but I assure you, it gets even more interesting. A few weeks later I ordered a pizza from a mom-and-pop chain, and the delivery guy turned out to be the student with the PDA. We were both a bit bewildered at first, trying to remember exactly how we knew each other. I asked about his paper, trying to imagine typing a two-thousand-word document on a mobile device, and he admitted that he was still having trouble doing the research. I grabbed my laptop, logged into a database, found a handful of articles, and e-mailed them to his account. He was impressed and very grateful and gave me my pizza for free.

A month later I ordered another pizza from the same restaurant and the same student delivered my food. He must have noted my name in the directory, because he arrived bearing free samples from the menu. This apparently was a bribe for me to help him with another class assignment. I had friends over that evening, so I was less inclined to help. I pulled a business card out of my wallet and told him that I could meet with him during the week. I could see from his expression, though, that he really needed help.

It was around this time that I was experimenting with social websites as a way to reach students online. Blogs, Facebook, MySpace, and similar websites offered new channels to interact with my user community. What I discovered was that interwoven throughout their digital conversations were many academic topics. Students turned to each other for help and guidance. They were asking each other reference questions: where to access articles, how to find books, and how to format citations. Despite classroom instruction, online tutorials, and promotional material, most students knew very little about the library. What was even more surprising was that many of these students actually visited the library regularly but had no clue how to use it or about the full range of tools and services available to them.

Entering this social sphere of students expanded my point of view. I was no longer bound behind the reference desk or limited by the classroom setting; instead, I could work with students by more naturally packaging the library into bite-size pieces as they needed it. I also found out more about what was happening around campus and starting attending activities such as guest lectures, special programs, exhibits, and sporting events. I ate lunch in the student center and walked around campus to see where people congregated. I also started talking more frequently with faculty and staff, not only about information literacy or scholarly communications, but about their research, their departments, and life on campus. I refer to this process as *becoming ubiquitous.* My mission wasn't to push the library's agenda, but rather to get involved on campus, to take an interest in what others were doing, and to offer my advice and assistance when they were needed. I didn't let the title of librarian define my involvement. I was no longer simply advocating for the library but instead doing what I could to help others become more successful. Obviously, with this growing empathic outlook I could not turn my back on the pizza delivery guy during his time of need.

This was about the time that ALA Editions contacted me about writing a book. They had come across some of my publications, read my blog, and were interested in the way that I communicated with students. I have pulled together a systematic approach; however, this is not a fill-in-the-blanks or color-by-number method. This book challenges you to think differently about the people we serve and the services that we offer. Granted, there is an enormous amount of published information on how libraries should market themselves, but I am grateful to have this opportunity to join the conversation. I won't make any claims that this is the best approach; it is simply what I have found works best for me.

1

Do Libraries Need to Advertise?

Let's be honest: libraries don't need to advertise. Perhaps it is unwise to introduce a marketing book with such a statement, but it's the truth. Students will always be drawn to the library: hunting for books buried away in the stacks, passing time between classes, cramming before a test, and yes, even hanging out with friends. Over the past decade there has been an enormous emphasis on *the library as place,* and we have seen the emergence of large computer labs, cafés, wireless Internet access, and comfortable furniture. These renovations have led to a tremendous surge in attendance, and in many cases libraries have become popular locations on campus. And so, if our buildings are filled, then why do we need to promote them? With gate counts and website hits rising, do we really need to invest time, money, and effort in advertising? While more and more students may be visiting the library, the real question is, are they aware of everything that we have to offer? Just because they are in our buildings doesn't necessarily mean that they are using library services effectively.

My objective is not to persuade you that libraries should embrace marketing methods, but rather to demonstrate the possibility of creating a richer library experience. *Marketing Today's Academic Library: A Bold New Approach to Communicating with Students* focuses on proactive and targeted communication strategies aimed at establishing an emotional and interactive connection with our users. By offering a balanced array of academic, social, creative, and cultural experiences, the library can become a premier campus destination, rather than just a place that students have to go. Instead of being grouped in with compulsory services such as the Department of Motor Vehicles, the post office, or financial aid, academic libraries can be a source of inspiration.

So how do we get there? This change in perception is not accomplished simply by plastering your library's logo, slogan, vision statement, or tagline on everything possible. A coffee mug, key-chain, or bookmark boasting about the size of your collection or your friendly customer service is not the answer either. You'll never change perceptions through countless committee meetings with discussions on value statements, strategic planning, or brand identity. Video games, iPods, DVDs, and other gimmicks are also not the solution. No, the process begins when we stop pretending that we know what students want and instead genuinely attempt to understand their needs and preferences—and speak to them in their language. We have to move beyond surveys, feedback forms, and contrived focus groups and embrace a wider tool kit of empathic and empathetic strategies. Instead of just paying lip service to a user-centered model, libraries must become user-sensitive organizations. This book takes the stance that promotional efforts must be social in nature, aimed at starting conversations instead of simply treating our users as a captive audience.

A SOCIAL APPROACH TO MARKETING

The term *social marketing* emerged in the early 1970s to raise the awareness of societal issues and to encourage social change. With the evolution of the Web, and particularly the interactivity of Web 2.0, social marketing has morphed into a communication method, rather than a description of the content. This book focuses on how academic libraries can build integrated promotional campaigns designed to be engaging. This is a shift away from the more traditional transaction-based approach and instead highlights the experiential narrative.

Most library advertising that targets undergraduates is based on promoting the collection, reference and instructional services, and occasional events such as guest speakers or exhibits. This narrow approach misses out on the big-picture potential. The guiding principle of this book is that library advertising should focus on the lifestyle of the user. We should show how the library fits within the daily life of our students, rather than the other way around. The library should not be viewed as a frightening or foreign location, but a productive, friendly, and supportive environment. We must demonstrate our value through applied relevance, instead of fabricating implied needs. On a grand scale, we need to stop thinking in terms of the user being in the library and instead consider how the library fits into the life of our users.

For example, let's say you want to promote your library's instant messenger (IM) service. You might place your account name on some pens to give away at the reference desk along with a few fliers at circulation, display it with a banner ad on the library's home page, mention it during instruction classes, and perhaps even add it to a Facebook profile. This approach is limited because it presupposes that students are either in the library or on your website and that they acknowledge the need to chat with a librarian.

Now let's consider a more social approach. I suggest designing an On My Buddy List campaign, highlighting several influential students that fit into different user segments (an artist, an athlete, and a popular fraternity member). Using a campuswide mixed media package, including web, print, and video content, show these students using the instant messenger service throughout the day: texting on a cell phone, late at night in a dorm, on a laptop during class, and even using a computer in the library. The context of these IM conversations should be humorous, informative, and relevant, highlighting a wide variety of library services, not just research assistance. I would also consider printing inexpensive napkins for the library café featuring intriguing questions and encouraging users to message the librarians in order to find out the answers. All students who use the service during a particular semester could also be entered into a monthly raffle as well. Additional coverage in the campus media outlets, such as newspaper, television, web portals, and radio, could also support the promotion.

This type of campaign demonstrates the value of the chat service by showcasing the user; students are the focus, not the librarian. It emphasizes the convenience of the chat reference with the actionable goal of convincing students to add the library account to their buddy list and ultimately to ask a question. By illustrating real-world questions and answers, students can envision themselves using the service as well. The objective is to introduce them to the library's services early in the semester, rather than at a point of frustration or anxiety. This campaign builds on the idea that the library is "on their buddy list" or within their circle of acquaintances so that wherever and whenever they need it, someone can help.

This shift toward experiential advertising moves us away from simply *telling* students what they should know about the library and instead *shows* them how the library applies to them. *Marketing Today's Academic Library* presents a tiered and incremental framework for building campaigns and delivering your message. The core attributes of this process include designing media packages that are tangible, experiential, relatable, measurable, shareable, and surprising. Promotional strategies must become participatory in order to have a meaningful and memorable impact on our audience.

PERSPECTIVES

The road to my experiential service perspective began in 1995 when as an undergraduate I shelved hundreds of books a day in my university's library. Students regularly approached me with questions; because I worked there, they perceived me to be a librarian. I was highly visible since I was out on the floors and could offer them instant assistance. Whenever they asked a question that I couldn't answer, I always suggested that they talk with a reference librarian, but students typically declined, preferring not to trouble themselves. This behavior subconsciously encouraged me to learn more about the library because I didn't like it when I was unable to provide help, or perhaps more accurately, I didn't want to look foolish in front of my peers.

I rediscovered these themes of convenience and peer support several years later as a reference librarian while reading student blogs. I noticed that students typically posed questions to their friends about finding information, writing papers, and many other academic subjects. I could see from these numerous posts and comments that very few of them were aware of all the services and resources that their libraries make available. Despite our instructional sessions, subject guides, tutorials, and gobs of promotional material, students simply didn't know about their library.

Fast-forward to 2007 when I became the user experience librarian at Georgia Tech. This unique position allows me to observe students and experiment with new ways of communicating library information. Simply put, my job is to make the library more visible, engaging, and accessible to our users. I spend a great deal of my time talking with students, not only about how they use the library, but about the challenges, frustrations, and triumphs they encounter in college. Thanks to Facebook, I have been able to extend this conversation beyond the halls of Georgia Tech and have interacted with hundreds of undergraduates across the United States. I have collected their stories, insights, suggestions, and problems in search of common threads. In addition to gathering this feedback, I conducted a study for the Association of Research Libraries on the topic of promoting libraries. This report provided me with a global perspective on how academic libraries organize, plan, and implement their marketing activities. When these two perspectives were combined, a juxtaposition emerged. In many ways librarians are disconnected from the undergraduates they serve; we are off base with our communication efforts. However, there are many opportunities before us in which we can start speaking their language.

MY JOURNEY INTO THE WORLD OF MARKETING

In preparation for this book, I tried to remove myself as much as I could from the *librarian mindset.* I unsubscribed from library electronic mailing lists, removed all library blogs from my aggregator, and for the most part stopped reading library journals. I even stepped down from my library's public relations committee and limited my involvement with ALA and ACRL. This intentional withdrawal allowed me to observe how libraries present themselves and, likewise, how users perceive libraries. By adopting this perspective, I could more clearly and critically evaluate the promotional efforts that libraries were making.

For nearly two years, I immersed myself in the *marketing mindset.* I didn't want to be on the inside looking out; that is, I didn't want to simply absorb business concepts and then try to forcibly apply them to the library work flow. Instead, I sought a much wider perspective; I needed to be on the outside looking in. I wanted to be able think like an advertiser and then approach the problem of promoting the library in that manner. My lofty goal was to transform the way that students perceived the library, not just how they used it.

During this submersion period I joined the Atlanta Interactive Marketing Association, which offers social events and regularly hosts high-profile speakers from companies such as Facebook, Google, Coca-Cola, Turner Broadcasting, UPS, Delta Air Lines, and MTV. I joined the American Marketing Association and regularly read *Ad Age,* as well as other business periodicals. I read countless marketing books, followed advertising blogs, and sat in on several business school course lectures. I visited bookstores and spent many hours flipping through magazines and newspapers studying the print ads. I also started watching television more frequently, particularly channels unfamiliar to me, simply to absorb the commercials. I even read every piece of junk mail sent to me, learning to appreciate the fine art of coupon crafting. Generally speaking, I became more attuned to all of the advertising messages that constantly surround us.

This mindset also affected me at work. I started walking around the campus more often and found myself eavesdropping on passing conversations, observing where students gathered, and obsessively collecting event fliers from student organizations. I started walking throughout the library daily to see how the space was being used, and I frequently worked at public computers. I needed to experience the library as the students did. This was an important step in order to be able to genuinely communicate with them. I needed to learn how to think like a student instead of a librarian pretending to know what users thought.

MY PITCH

Most libraries are already involved in some form of advertising. Although we refer to it by different names including outreach, communication, advocacy, or public relations, academic libraries are unquestionably trying to reach their students. But is it working? My research reveals that most of these efforts are inconsistent, fragmented, and largely go without assessment. My stance is that if you're going to promote the library, then why not approach it like a marketing executive?

This book provides you with a framework for designing messages that are targeted at desired results and outcomes. I offer practical and tested strategies that all types and sizes of academic libraries can use. The book is not meant to be a blueprint or a step-by-step guide, but rather a starting point for conversations between you and your library staff. In these pages, I share with you the system that I have developed over thirteen years of working in academic libraries and obsessively studying the culture of marketing. As we know, all student populations are different, and what works well for one library may not work well at another; your challenge is to find the voice that speaks to your users. I hope that I can help.

2

Defining the User

What are *they* doing in *our* libraries? Many academic libraries are showing an upward trend in gate counts, but just what exactly are students doing in our buildings?

- waiting for a friend
- checking e-mail
- watching YouTube videos
- burning a CD
- playing Yahoo! games
- recharging an iPod
- grabbing lunch
- printing out boarding passes
- taking a nap
- photocopying fliers

These activities don't make it into our strategic plans, nor do they fit into the lofty mission and vision statements of the typical academic library. While we strive for nobler pursuits, such as building collections or teaching information literacy, library users live in a different world. For them the library is merely a stop along the way of a very busy day. Students constantly juggle complex social, personal, and academic responsibilities; if we want to communicate with them, then we have to recognize how the library fits within their lifestyle. However, before we even begin to tell our story, we have to know to whom we are talking. This chapter places the student in the forefront.

WHO ARE THEY?

If we truly aspire to create user-centered libraries, then let's begin by scratching out the word *patron.* Yes, tuition technically may support the library budget, but this does not constitute a true benefactor relationship. And I'm not including those *mandatory* fees that some libraries collect. Students are not intentionally entrusting libraries with their tuition dollars in the same way that an artist is commissioned for a portrait. If anything, our campus administrators are the real patrons; they are the ones handing over the funding and investing in our work.

Instead of *patron,* let's try a more accurate label such as *customer, user, audience, group, class, community member, segment, student, professor, faculty, staff member, donor,* or *alumni.* Those are the terms I use throughout this book. To some librarians *customer* is a dirty word; it somehow belittles what we do. But in all honesty, it is the customer-supplier relationship that best describes the transactions of the typical academic library. We offer them a product or service, and they in turn choose to use it or not.

Honestly, though, it doesn't matter what we call them because we treat them as spectators. They are the wildlife in the academic jungle that we observe safely from behind our desks. Ask your students if they feel that your library is user-centered and they will probably say no. Actually, they would probably be confused by the question since libraries have a long tradition of being prohibitive places. The thought of the users having a say in matters is incomprehensible. But our behind-the-scenes operations are not transparent to them. Numerous students have told me they don't see the business side of the library or any other campus facilities, such as the gym, housing, or the student center; they simply expect good, clean facilities that work properly.

Our challenge then is to come out from behind the desk, both physically and philosophically, and create engaging library experiences. Outreach has to be more than simply showing and telling. We have to cast aside the librarian-knows-best mentality that comes across as *eat your vegetables* and *take your vitamins* and instead treat our users as partners in the educational process. Our goal should be focused on the objective of student success. In fact, being user-centered is probably not enough.

It is a user-sensitive library, one with genuine interest and concern toward its users that builds an ongoing and beneficial relationship.

Bear in mind that college is a complex duality of excitement and stress. It is a major, life-changing transformation fueled by intense pressure and high expectations. And it's not all just about attending class, writing papers, and doing research; let's not forget about the leisure activities, sports, cultural events, clubs and organizations, community service, socializing, romance, rivalries, roommates, and many other aspects contributing to this growth phase. Somewhere in all this commotion is the library. And it may be hard for us to break away from the library-centered universe, but there is more to college than academics, just as there is more to libraries than circulation stats and gate counts. We are all part of the larger campus ecosystem. We should not limit our efforts to promoting the reference desk or a new database, but instead be focused on *improving the quality of life* on campus.

To begin this conversation, we have to define our users more clearly, widening our perspective and affording us the ability to zero in on particular needs. In studying the following characteristics and trends, opportunities emerge for librarians to communicate with our user population more effectively.

THE TWENTY-FOUR-HOUR LIFE CYCLE

When does the majority of your library staff work? From nine in the morning to five at night? While this schedule may be convenient for us, it is not prime time for students. While they're in class, eating lunch, working, or attending activities, librarians are standing by. I've often heard the argument that if students truly need help, then they will make an appointment. This notion implies that they should make time for us, fitting their needs into our schedules, just like they do for banks, mechanics, or physicians. However, a nine-to-five library schedule is not optimal because it's not when they're focused on schoolwork. So what exactly are students doing with their time?[1]

In the mornings and afternoons, students are on the go. Library visits are juggled between other activities, and students are in a constant state of multitasking. During this time, there is a much greater demand for express services, such as quick printing, e-mailing, picking up books, or asking basic questions. This time period is also filled with last-minute reviewing before a test or relaxing between classes. The library serves as a pit stop, a refueling station before returning to the business of the day.

The evening hours, however, reveal a much different mood. While students still have a lot on their minds, they are much less confined by other obligations. They can devote more time to assignments. In fact, many students I have spoken with indicated that when they come to the library at night, they intend to stay for a long time. They consciously have to pack up the necessary supplies, such as textbooks, notebooks, food, sweaters, laptops, and other essential items, and then make the journey to the library. Once they are there, they intend to work.

I've always found this dichotomy of day and night personalities to be evident in how students approach the reference desk. Day users tend to be slightly impatient; they want to locate particular information right away. They are typically confined by a timetable and are trying to fit us in. However, students in the evening tend to be much more receptive to instructional efforts. They are more likely to ask questions and can take the time to understand how our systems work. It is important to keep this in mind as we begin forming communication strategies. Developing a great message is one thing, but timing is crucial. The student that we encounter in the library at ten o'clock in the morning will be in a different state of mind at ten at night. There are twenty-four hours in a day, so we shouldn't limit ourselves to the nine-to-five mentality. Otherwise we may be missing out on an opportunity when students are more open to learning about the library.

SEMESTER PROGRESSION

Have you ever noticed the mood during the first few weeks of each semester? There is an abundance of enthusiasm: new classes, new expectations, new professors, and new classmates. It is a fresh start. Now fast-forward several weeks and the tone is much different. Everything is serious; the first test has been taken, assignments are under way, and something is always due next week. It doesn't take long for students to establish their new routines, with everything building toward the crescendo of finals week.

This is the cycle of academic life. Each day is progress along the path to completion. This sequence is very visible within the library. You can easily observe the mounting intensity as deadlines arise. A student who is sipping coffee in the café one day is later hidden away in the stacks. Long lines form around the printers, groups wander looking for an open place to study, and the pace of academic activity increases.

This blossoming of the semester is important to keep in mind when designing communications. The tone of messages that we use at the beginning of the term is probably less effective as the weeks advance down. However, understanding the progression of this scholarly flow is helpful because we can take advantage of it accordingly. Each semester is highly predictable; we know when it begins and when it ends, and in between are the assignments, tests, midterms, and finals, as well as holidays and breaks. Everything revolves around fixed periods and due dates, which benefits us because we can anticipate needs.

Let's think about the structure of the semester in terms of the annual holidays. If you walk through any department store in October, you'll probably see a special section devoted to Halloween costumes and candy. Later in the year Christmas is the dominant theme. Valentine's Day brings hearts and chocolate, Mother's Day features flowers, and Independence Day is heralded by barbecue supplies and flags. Each holiday is associated with particular traditions, customs, and activities, requiring a specific set of goods and services. Grocery and department stores can anticipate when we need turkey basters and pumpkin pies and present these items in seasonal displays. They maximize their profits while saving our time and giving us what they know we need.

Libraries can adopt this strategy as well. The beginning of the school year is the ideal time for a casual introduction with food, games and fun, tours and orientations. Our goal is to gain visibility. As the semester progresses, our message shifts to emphasize the productivity aspects of the library: the demonstration of our products and services and the value they provide. As the semester wraps up, the library plays a support role with extended hours, study space, and food for refueling; it is a battle station for finals.

This process works with instruction as well. By collecting course syllabi, we can predict the types of questions, problems, and projects that students will encounter. Instead of trying to teach students everything at once, we can dole out what they need to know as they move through each semester. For example, I know that during the fourth week of every semester at Georgia Tech, many mechanical engineering students develop a sudden interest in patents and safety standards for a senior design class. Being able to anticipate this need, I can arrange my schedule to offer on-the-fly training, as well as make appearances in the classroom and provide my colleagues at the reference desk with tips for using these resources.

By targeting these opportune times, we can integrate seamlessly into the semester flow and position ourselves as a solutions provider. Take a look at what's going on around campus week after week and find a way to participate. During summer orientations when many parents are on campus, offer them a library breakfast.[2] Over homecoming week when many alumni return, offer a networking or cultural program for them. From Earth Day to Election Day, partnering opportunities are always present. This is big-picture thinking, always considering how you can get involved around campus with various student clubs or academic departments. Just as we schedule our holidays and vacations, the semester can be broken into micro-components with associated needs, moods, and activities. We'll examine this notion of timing in more detail in chapter 9, but the core concept is that we can actively seek to interweave the library across the semester. By anticipating needs, our communications can evolve along with our users as we present library products, services, and spaces in a relevant, intuitive, and immediate manner.

USER FREQUENCY

Why is it that some students seem to live in the library while others have no idea where it is? Marketing dogma states that it is much easier to keep a current customer than it is to convert a new one, so why don't we apply this principle as well? The library literature, electronic mailing lists, blogs, message boards, poster sessions, and conference presentations are filled with ideas for convincing students to use our services. However, very little attention, if any, is devoted to enhancing the experience of students already familiar with the library. If you think about it in commercial terms, consider the difference between a loyal consumer and the occasional one. Companies often create incentives for their regular customers. Coca-Cola offers reward points that can be redeemed for gifts; Hampton Inn favors business travelers with special rates. Are we missing out on the opportunity to build stronger relationships with our heaviest users because we are too distracted trying to reach new ones?

In academic libraries, we treat all students the same. This practice is a flaw on our part because they are not equal. Don't get me wrong, everyone is entitled to the same level of access, courtesy, and professionalism, but from a marketing perspective all people should not be lumped together. If you sell kitchen appliances, your pitch to a chef is not the same as to the casual cook. A car dealer uses a different approach when showcasing a luxury car than he would an economy vehicle. I am not arguing that we should stop recruiting new customers, but only that we need to pay equal attention to the ones we already have.

To further illustrate this concept and provide a common language, I have created several generalized categories of users based on their frequency of library visits. These labels are not scientific and might not apply to all libraries; they are simply intended to serve as an organizational aid for brainstorming. These are the terms that I personally use to differentiate students.

The Connoisseurs. This group has a profound appreciation for libraries. They know how to search the databases and turn to them often. Connoisseurs are expert users, and they are quick to make suggestions or point out when something is wrong or out of place. Their visits will vary, but to them the library is first and foremost a research tool. Compared to the other groups, connoisseurs have higher expectations, and perhaps unrealistic desires, of what the library should be. They can also be its biggest advocates and will mention the library with glowing esteem.

The Regulars. These students are in the library daily or at least several times a week. They tend to have more of a scholarly bent than the average student, investing a great deal of time in their readings and assignments. For them the library is a destination, a place that is both part of their standard routine and an outlet for social and scholarly activities. However, just because they are in the building doesn't mean that they are aware of everything that the library has to offer.

Irregular Guests. These students only go to the library when they have to. They are occasional visitors who use the library for a particular function: studying before a test, meeting with a group, or checking out a book on course reserve. Guests do not drop by for pleasure; for them the library is like a chore or an errand—something that has to be done.

The Vacationers. These students typically use the library as a resting stop during the day; it is a convenient place to check e-mail, grab a coffee, meet a friend, and perhaps glance over a textbook. Individuals in this group don't really consider themselves to be library patrons but more like accidental visitors who happened to wander in.

The Invisibles. You know that guy who brags about graduating without ever having set foot into the library? Well, this is that guy. These students simply have no interest in the library, or rather in what they perceive the library has to offer, no matter what we have to say about it.

Undoubtedly these categories oversimplify our user population. They are not intended to be definitive, but simply to provide a framework for imagining usage. Let's say that you intend to renovate. How would your plans impact each of these groups? Elements that might be attractive to some will be less appealing, or possibly even off-putting, to others. Now apply this method to your advertising campaigns. Each student perceives the library differently; some want to hear about databases and resources, while some are more interested in multimedia software and DVDs and others in guest speakers, film viewings, or café specials. Your challenge is to find out what motivates particular users and then deliver the information they want to hear in a way that works for them. Student usage of the library is varied, and we can't expect one message to appeal to everyone.

USER SEGMENTATION

The most effective way to tell someone about the library is face to face. When I offer research consultations, students are impressed with the wide array of available resources and often leave with a positive outlook toward their assignment. Librarians serve to make the library relevant; we can translate the value to users on a personal level. We are able to listen to their unique questions and respond with customized advice and recommendations. The problem, though, is that one-on-one interaction is not an efficient communication method. You can't get direct face time with all of your students.

We're not alone in this task; in fact, it is one of the central challenges that most enterprises face. Regardless of the industry, the ability to deliver a targeted message to the right person at the right time is difficult. While companies have the advantage of larger advertising budgets and an army of staff dedicated to studying consumers, academic libraries benefit from the close proximity to their populations. It is much easier for us to observe, experiment, interact, and react to our users.

In order to increase the effectiveness of communication efforts, librarians can adopt the practice of segmentation, the process of grouping people together based on similar characteristics that result in comparable needs. This practice is similar to the user frequency groupings introduced previously, although those classifications are a bit abstract. Segmentation allows us more precision in narrowing down our audience.

Think about segmentation in terms of geography; residents in the northern states have very different apparel needs than southerners, especially during winter months. Demographically, senior citizens have a different set of needs and priorities than teenagers. And although not all teenagers have the same interests, tastes, or behavior, segmentation increases the chance of messages being more on target. By placing our students into groups with similar characteristics, we can potentially increase the likelihood of crafting a relevant promotional campaign.

We can carve up our populations in numerous ways. In fact, many librarians are already performing this type of outreach. By applying basic segmentation approaches to our promotional efforts, we can focus deeper and, ideally, be more relevant. Let's start by looking at several groups commonly found within the academic community.

Segmentation by Year

The most common form of segmentation in higher education is by academic year: freshmen, sophomores, juniors, and seniors. Each group is loosely tied to a series of collective experiences that are shaped by academic progression—the grand conveyer belt moving students toward the goal of graduation. With each passing semester, students become more familiar with campus culture. They learn which professors to take or avoid, how to set up their schedule and manage their time, and all the good places to eat. They also encounter the library.

Academic libraries place a lot of emphasis on freshmen. The premise is that if we can reach them early, then they will continue to use the library. Once we get them through the door and accustomed to visiting the library, they will discover additional services they need. Freshmen are commonly targeted through welcome events and activities, orientations, and tours. Some libraries even hire a first-year instruction liaison dedicated to teaching this segment. Ironically, even with all this attention, most freshmen view the library as a large study hall and computer lab. During the initial semester their information needs are minimal, other than a few articles for English papers and perhaps some reserve readings. While academic librarians are focused on information literacy, it isn't until much later that students typically have more advanced research needs.

After the initial year, library outreach becomes less consistent. While some courses lend themselves to library experiences, many do not. Additionally, some disciplines are more library-friendly than others. This challenge of integrating the library into the curriculum is a common one for the profession. Although librarians may be eager to instruct, classroom face time is not always available. Faculty may want students to use library resources, but they're not always willing to forfeit class time. This predicament leaves us with the challenge of finding creative ways to increase awareness of the library's value.

Other factors influence this scheme of academic segmentation. Not all students arrive on campus as freshmen. Distance learners are often out of sight and therefore out of mind. This hidden group is mostly interested in collections, particularly full-text resources, but they generally welcome instruction. Other than the online interactions they have with professors and classmates, the library is often their sole connection to the campus. Transfer students represent another segment that deserves attention, since they miss out on the early discovery experiences traditionally afforded during freshman year. These students are constantly trying to catch up to their peers and must quickly adapt to campus culture. Part of their readjustment period includes figuring out the library. Similarly, adult learners, or the ill-named *nontraditional students,* are retuning to college after an absence. Some time may have elapsed since they last used a library, and undoubtedly things have changed.

Segmentation by Discipline

Another common form of segmentation is by discipline. Academic libraries have long used the subject liaison model to divide responsibilities of expertise. By placing students together by major, we can present the library to them as a customized package. For example, students studying chemistry require a different set of tools than those majoring in economics, just as humanities majors will rely on a different set of resources than those studying engineering. From this view, our collections, databases, and software are perceived very distinctly; some disciplines rely more heavily on the library than others, and the tool kit that one group uses will be of little interest to others. This fragmentation can lead to varied opinions toward the library; some majors will be better supported than others. But by using a discipline segmentation approach, librarians can focus and align resources with particular courses or assignments, making the library a seamless part of the academic experience.

Social Segmentation

Psychodemographics or social segmentation is a marketing approach that is largely underutilized by academic libraries. This method classifies groups based on lifestyle, personal outlook, behaviors, or aspirations. The objective is to place individuals together who think or act similarly. For example, people of the same age and tax bracket, living in the same geographic location, do not necessarily share the same interests. However, men belonging to the same country club will likely share common values. Single, thirty-something women living in a particular metro area may not have comparable lifestyles, whereas women who regularly visit Starbucks, eat organic food, attend yoga classes, use MacBooks, drive VWs, and read the *New York Times* probably share a similar political and social outlook.

Demographics can describe a given population, but psychodemographics reveal more about who the members are. Of course this approach is not a perfect science, and there is a definite danger of stereotyping. However, librarians can use this technique when designing promotional campaigns by appealing to different lifestyles. People prefer to hang out with their friends and study together as well. These personal connections within psychodemographics enable us to use word-of-mouth methods to spread awareness. By getting students talking about the library, we increase the likelihood that they will use it. Let's look at several of the most common social groups that can be found around campus.

Greeks

Most colleges support a number of fraternities and sororities that make up the Greek community. These large social networks center around smaller subsets or cliques of close friends. Such organizations tend to be bureaucratic and often include a scholarship chair and a public relations coordinator. These two positions are valuable connections, making the spread of information easier within the tightly contained groups. But aside from simply pushing out information to them, we should treat the Greek organizations as a vital campus ally. Taking into consideration the philanthropic and community service–oriented missions of fraternities and sororities, libraries can greatly benefit by gaining Greek support.

Geeks, Gamers, and Gadget Guys

If the Greeks are the social butterflies on campus, then this group is their opposite. Stereotypically drawn to hobbies such as video games, comic books, and science fiction, geeks are more introspective. However, their eccentric interests, creativity, and intellectual bent make them ideal library users. By offering events and displays specifically for them, and using imaginative advertising, the library can offer much to this segment.

Athletes

Student-athletes spend an enormous amount of their time in practice and traveling to competitions. Because of their busy schedules, athletes often have predefined study times and often study together. Library use varies from school to school and sport to sport. Some programs offer this group private study centers and tutors, while others require a quota of time spent in the library. Outreach to this segment should focus on the advisors who look after the athletes' academic needs. In several ways this group is similar to distance learners, and librarians should accordingly highlight resources and services that can be used remotely. From an advertising stance, athletes make great spokespersons since they are highly visible; however, due to their demands they are not always available. Additionally, NCAA regulations and the Athletic Association can present numerous challenges that make it difficult to include athletes in promotional material.

Activists

Library mission statements often mention libraries' being the intellectual and cultural centers of campus. To achieve this, libraries need more than robust collections; they must also offer a forum for the open exchange of ideas. This philosophy ties into the activist segment on campus, composed of organizations with social, political, or environmental agendas. The library can serve these groups as a showcase, meeting ground, and information channel. By catering to these students and providing them with engagement opportunities, the library subsequently becomes a hub of activity.

Artists

These are the painters, poets, musicians, graphic designers, actors, and architects on campus. They tend to have strong emotional ties to the library, since it is a traditional icon of the humanities. Students in this segment congregate in tight-knit groups, often with others who share artistic talents. The best way to reach these users is to celebrate the creative spirit and to highlight resources that would help them advance their craft. Similar to the activists, this segment can be enticed by events and exhibits; turn the library into their canvas and allow them to discuss and display their works.

Student Government and Leaders

Student government members are the elected leaders on campus, the voice of the student body. Of course there are others who take on leadership responsibilities, such as the presidents or organizers of campus clubs, groups, and associations, but those units tend to fall under the umbrella of the Student Government Association (SGA). Student leaders are great allies; they tend to be ambitious, invested, well connected, and generally willing to work with departments on campus. Keep these students in the loop with library news and changes and solicit their feedback. In turn they'll spread the word to others and feel involved in the process. Although student leaders are easy to track down, they tend to be very involved, and hence their schedules are often stretched thin.

International and Minority Students

The composition of this segment will vary from school to school. Obviously there are many differences between cultures, and these students should not be simply lumped together in a giant *other* category. However, international and minority students typically form strong bonds, relying on each other for support and socialization. Many international students view the library as neutral and common ground on campus. Librarians can leverage their diversity with specialized instruction sessions and events.

Segmentation is a valuable tool for librarians. Instead of designing promotions for the broadest audience possible, sorting our patrons into various categories enables us to target niche groups and provide timely, relevant, and personalized messages.

STUDENT LIFE STAGES

Famed psychologist Erik Erikson wrote extensively about the natural stages of human life from childhood to adolescence, through adulthood, middle, and old age. These developmental periods shape our roles and identities, influencing how we perceive and interact within society. There are also several common events that people experience, such as graduating from high school, buying a house, starting a new job, getting married, having a baby, and retiring. As we mature, our outlook and priorities shift regarding aspects such as finances, family, health, religion, and leisure time. Life is a constant and gradual accumulation of these universal experiences.

The same concept applies to higher education. The college experience is often regarded as one of the defining periods in a person's life; it is one transition into adulthood. However, this complex stage actually includes several independent phases.[3] Awareness of these emotional and developmental periods can aid librarians with marketing, as well as instruction, event planning, service and resources allocation, and other engagement opportunities. Let's review the various stages that college students encounter.

Pre-freshmen (Anticipation). Once they are accepted but before they move in, students are in the pre-freshmen phase. This next step after high school is met with a mixture of excitement and anxiety. The group has many questions and fears as they enter into a culture in which they must adopt new customs and attitudes. The library's message at this time should be welcoming and reassuring.

First-Semester Freshmen (Adaptation). Entering freshmen face a great adjustment. This is the phase when college becomes real and boundaries are tested. All their lives they have heard about the college lifestyle, and the initial semester serves as their indoctrination. Peers now become their major influence, and along with that come new pressures. During this period, students encounter many social, academic, and personal expectations. The library's message is inviting, with a hint of what is to come.

Second-Semester Freshmen—Junior (Incubation). After the initial semester, students settle into their new routine. This phase marks a shift toward introspection, in which students are figuring out what they want from college as well as life; the anecdotal *finding oneself.* During this transformation, students reassess themselves, their friends, and their values. They start to branch out and explore new ideas, typically through involvement in student clubs and organizations. The library becomes a melting pot of ideas, scholarship, friendships, and experiences.

Juniors and Seniors (Actualization). At this phase students have passed through initiation and are now embedded in campus culture. Not only do they understand how the system works, but they become a core part of it. They are very influential socially, the movers and shakers on campus. And academically they are deep into their discipline studies. For these students the end is in sight, and they start to tip toward completion. The library is a laboratory for getting work done.

Final-Semester Seniors (Anticipation). At this final phase students come full circle, mirroring the so-called senioritis they had in high school. They are conscious that the college experience is ending and that they are moving on to the ambiguous real world. During their final semester, students typically pull back from campus culture, although they may be nostalgic for past times. They recognize that they have endured and are now focused on finishing up and moving on to the next stage of life. At this stage, the library should be a reflection on past success.

APPLYING USER-CENTERED THINKING

Just as students are unique in encountering college at different stages, the way they use the library is different as well. Their academic progression should factor into our promotional strategy. If we limit ourselves to traditional big-message marketing, then we may miss out on opportunities to reach niche groups with specialized needs. If we only focus on freshman English courses, then students may never gain exposure to all the benefits that their library has to offer. There is more to college than writing papers, just as there is more to libraries than online databases. Our students are multifaceted, and so too should be our communication initiatives.

Let's look at an example of how the concepts in this chapter can be applied. Incoming freshmen often feel nervous about midterms and finals. They want to do well in their first semester. Most of them are taking the same core courses and therefore have tests around the same time. The library can help alleviate their anxiety by offering coordinated study sessions and bringing together teaching assistants, tutors, and upperclassmen to host regular review sessions for many of the general education courses. These informal sessions both target specific academic needs and serve as a social component for peer mentoring. This type of encounter plants the idea that the library is more than just a computer lab or a place for books; it is directly linked to classroom success. They were probably already going to study anyway, but in this manner the library becomes integrated into their lifestyle. This is empathic thinking; instead of just trying to imagine ways to get more students to use the library, we flip the question around and ask, what do students need this week and how might the library help provide it?

The above example emphasizes the true value of the library and moves us in the direction of becoming a user-sensitive organization. While we might focus on specific duties, such as collection development, instruction, cataloging, systems, or borrowing privileges, the real issue is student success. Although there are many other service-oriented buildings on campus—the dining hall, the gym, the bookstore, and the student center—the library is the only one that connotes neutral ground. It is an open (and ideally inviting) location where students from all segments come together for a variety of purposes. The library symbolizes more than just a place; it is not just the collections of books and journals, computers and study carrels, or even the research help that define it. It is the less tangible qualities that truly distinguish its value: motivation, confidence, and creativity. We'll explore this further in chapter 7, but next let's continue to examine our customers by digging deeper into understanding their needs.

NOTES

1. Bureau of Labor Statistics, "Time Use on an Average Weekday for Full-Time University and College Students," www.bls.gov/tus/charts/students.htm; Peter Dolton, Oscar Marcenaro, and Lucia Navarro, "The Effective Use of Student Time," *Economics of Education Review* 22 (Dec 2003): 547–60; Sarath Nonis and Gail Hudson, "Academic Performance of College Students: Influence of Time Spent Studying and Working," *Journal of Education for Business* 81 (Jan/Feb 2006): 151–59.

2. Nancy Foster and Susan Gibbons, eds., *Studying Students: The Undergraduate Research Project at the University of Rochester* (Chicago: Association of College and Research Libraries, 2008).
3. William Perry, *Forms of Intellectual and Ethical Development in the College Years: A Scheme* (New York: Holt, Rinehart, and Winston, 1968); E. Marilyn Schaeffer and Maribeth Durst, "Phases, Not Stages: The Life Cycle of College Students," *College Student Affairs Journal* 9 (1989): 31–37; Thomas Good and Jere Brophy, *Educational Psychology: A Realistic Approach* (New York: Longman, 1990).

3

Student Need States

When I lived in the Washington, D.C., metro area, I frequently ate lunch at Così. This gourmet sandwich bistro has several convenient locations, an interesting menu, and efficient on-the-go service; it's an ideal place for the busy lunch hour. One evening I ate dinner there, and to my surprise it was a completely different experience. Instead of several clusters of small tables, the furniture was arranged to accommodate groups; instead of standing in line to order, there was a waitstaff. Dinner also featured wine, music, and mood lighting. Così adapts to the needs of their customers based on the time of day; at midday the bistros provide a quick lunch, while in the evening they expand the menu and emphasize the atmosphere.

We can apply the same principle to libraries. We know that students need different things at different times of the day, as well as at specific points of time throughout the semester. Our challenge then is to align our products and services to be more optimal. What is it that students need in the morning, compared with the afternoon or late evening? A student asking a reference question during the day most likely has a different mindset than one seeking help at night: Is he on his way to class or did he just get off work? Is he on his way to lunch or did he just eat dinner? Is his assignment due next week or is it due tomorrow? Obviously it is impossible for us to account for all possible variations; however, anyone who has worked at a public service desk for several years recognizes patterns that emerge throughout the school year. By anticipating these patterns and building them into our communication strategy, librarians are better positioned to support users.

This chapter uncovers and categorizes the needs that typical students encounter. The goal is to understand not only how they perceive the library, but also the big-picture challenges that they face in college, and then to work toward filling those gaps in perception. This is a critical step in the communication process as we strive to match library products with customer needs. Once this foundation is in place, you can begin designing promotional strategies that effectively demonstrate the value of your library.

NEED STATES

What do students need? My advice is to start from scratch when trying to answer this question. Forget everything that you assume about the library. In fact, leave your survey results, gate counts, feedback comments, LibQUAL+ data, and any other reports on your desk and take a walk around the building. Spend time with your population; observe them. How do they interact with each other, with library staff, with print resources, and with the environment? A person isn't just studying; he is tucked away in a quiet corner, hidden and possessive of his surrounding space. A group doesn't just sit together; they socialize, tutor, collaborate, and possibly motivate each other. Perhaps the most important question we can ask is *why*? Why are they using the library? What particular need is being fulfilled?

In the marketing industry there is a growing emphasis on the concept of need states. These mental states are described as psychological or functional conditions that can be aligned with purchases, such as grooming, beauty, or snacks, as well as with objectives, such as making dinner, taking care of a child, or getting ready for work.[1] By understanding the purpose of the shopping encounter, retailers can package items that directly match customer needs. Think of everything that you need for serving Thanksgiving dinner, taking a trip to the beach, or fighting the flu. These events aren't just activities, they are emotional experiences: Thanksgiving is about family, the beach is about relaxation, and the flu is about recovery.

We are constantly transitioning from one need state to another, even when we eat. A study of restaurants found that people choose different locations depending on various occasions, such as a romantic evening or being in a hurry.[2] They do not simply want good Italian food, but a first date or an anniversary experience. Restaurant selection depends on more than just what is on the menu; also in play are the mood of customers and the desire they want to satisfy. Someone who is grabbing dinner after work will most likely seek different culinary qualities than someone dining with friends after a movie.

The Dairy Association has also explored need states by investigating instances of beverage consumption throughout the typical day.[3] This study identified several need states, such as refreshment/thirst quenching, awake/energy, social, comfort/indulgence, meal replacement, and health-focused. By understanding why and when people consume a variety of beverages, the milk industry hopes to position their products as a more obvious choice to consumers. Their goal is to be able to offer a portfolio of milk-based beverages targeted for each need: a dairy-based drink designed for social activities, another for comfort, another for energy, and so forth.

Similarly, Coca-Cola has also explored the need state concept, hoping to transform from a soda-centric organization into a broader beverage provider. Instead of simply repackaging existing drinks in slightly new flavors, they are aiming to create new types of beverages. The Coca-Cola marketing team has identified several primal need states, including hunger and digestion, mental renewal, and health and beauty, and is experimenting with drinks that meet each of these conditions.[4] In the future, they hope to provide drinks that are fortified with vitamins and nutrients and provide the same benefits as a facial scrub or cold cream. Their ultimate goal is to sell drinks that make you not only feel better, but also become healthier. In the future, we won't just partake in a beverage because we're thirsty, but also to gain additional benefits.

STUDENT NEED STATES

Need states are also present in the academic environment. Students moving throughout the day develop a wide variety of obligations. Librarians can benefit by acknowledging these needs and aligning our services to address each one. Just as companies bundle products together to satisfy an intended purpose, libraries can also expand their reach on student time. In chapter 2 we examined the semester flow and twenty-four-hour life cycle of the college student; here I will introduce seven categories representing the broad spectrum of student needs.

Academic Needs. Not only do students spend several hours a week in the classroom, but they also attend labs, recitation, office hours, and reviews. Outside of these formal activities, students also attend informal study sessions, review textbooks and notes, practice presentations, and perform numerous other assignment-related tasks. Their academic responsibilities are an omnipresent part of their life.

Social Needs. While academic needs may dominate the student schedule, social activities are also important. From hanging out with friends or developing romantic relationships, to talking with family on the phone or attending parties, students engage in a variety of social encounters. Some students are highly socially occupied, such as those belonging to the Greek community or involved with campus clubs and organizations, while other students prefer to interact with a small group of friends. Social opportunities fluctuate throughout the semester; however, the need for companionship, mentorship, and camaraderie is a driving factor for many students.

Entertainment and Recreational Needs. Entertainment and recreation is another common theme, covering a wide range of activities such as leisure reading, creative expression, cultural exposure, hobbies, games, concerts, movies and television, sporting events, and exercise. While many of these outings are social in nature, they are focused on particular activities, elevating the experience above a mere conversational encounter.

Service Needs. A commitment to service is present in many students' lives. This can take the form of employment or volunteerism with groups such as Habitat for Humanity or campus organizations. Opportunities abound for participation in charity, religious, environmental, civic, political, and professional activities.

Personal Needs. Students have a variety of personal needs: hygiene, shopping, cleaning, laundry, managing finances, medical visits, and numerous other chores, errands, and responsibilities. Personal time is also necessary for reflection, meditation, assessing priorities, and planning.

Travel Needs. A surprising amount of students' time is spent moving from point A to point B. From home, to class, to work, to a friend's house, they are in constant motion. The modes of transportation may include cars, buses, and bikes, but most of the time is spent walking. Added to this is the incredible amount of supplies that students need to carry around with them: books, laptops, food, clothing, cell phones, MP3 players, keys, notebooks, and school supplies.

Rejuvenation Needs. With such a breadth of activities packed into each day, sometimes students just need to unwind. Rest and relaxation occurs when possible; however, eight hours of continuous sleep is highly uncommon. Food consumption is similarly scattered, typically fitting in when convenient. With the on-the-go lifestyle, many students rely on naps and snacks to refresh, refuel, and replenish before returning to action.

While there are certainly other demands, these categories represent the major components that all students require. To be user-sensitive organizations, we must visualize how a trip to the library fits in with everything else they have going on. Similar to the Dairy Association's objective of pushing milk-based products into new domains, librarians should integrate their products into the student lifestyle. How can we provide opportunities for students to fulfill social, entertainment, or service needs? To be user-centered, a library has to be more than just a great channel for academic services; it should provide a rich atmosphere that supports cultural, social, leisure, and creative activities as well. Students cannot be expected to study for several hours without an opportunity to revitalize both their body and mind. Libraries need to provide a variety of study environments ranging from quiet to noisy, from comfortable to rigid, from isolated to communal. A visit to the library should not be limited to fulfilling research needs but should allow opportunities to grab a snack, gossip with friends, take a nap, watch a movie, or listen to a motivating speaker. If our goal is to increase student usage and time spent in the library, then we have to focus constantly on student need fulfillment by offering a diversity of spaces, programming, products, services, and experiences, each designed to accommodate their shifting moods and priorities. In short, we need to give them new reasons to use the library.

This concept of filling the need will factor largely into our messaging. We can present the library in many different ways: instead of just for doing research, it is the place to start, revise, and finish an assignment. It is a pit stop during the day and a quiet couch late in the afternoon. It is a place to plug in literally to the Web and figuratively to new ideas, advice, and experiences. The library is a shrine of solitude, designed for introspection, discovery, and preparation. And it is also a social hub, filled with friends, activities, surprises, and chance encounters. Our central theme should be that the library is the place where things happen on campus, and our promotional efforts should align with these various need states. In this way, students won't need to think about why they should use the library but instead will simply see it as the logical destination. In the next chapter we will start assembling the product portfolio: what exactly is it that your library has to offer?

NOTES

1. Ted Taft, "Retail Reinvented," *The Hub* (May/June 2006): 10–11.
2. Bruce Tait, "The Increasing Importance of a Portfolio in a World of Decreasing Brand Loyalty," www.iconocast.com/ZZZZZResearch_Files/increasing_importance.pdf.
3. Dairy Management Inc., "Making Milk the Obvious Choice," *Tools for Innovation* 1 (Fall 2006).
4. Dean Foust, "Queen of Pop," *Business Week*, August 7, 2008.

4 The Library as Product

Each summer I randomly poll twenty incoming freshmen about their anticipation of starting college. One of the questions I ask is, what do you expect to find in an academic library? Overwhelmingly, and yet not surprisingly, students mention books and research material. Other consistent responses are nooks and crannies for studying, quiet reading rooms, and comfortable places to sit. Beyond resources and spaces, students also occasionally mention getting help, friendly staff, and a studious atmosphere. All of these elements are products; this is what we offer. By conceptualizing the library as a marketplace and matching our services to user needs, our communication strategies become more targeted. This chapter introduces a product-oriented framework that will help us organize and package library services, making them easier to promote.

DEFINING THE PRODUCT

We commonly think of products as objects that are mass-produced and sold in stores: gadgets, clothing, food, or soap. However, products are much more than such tangibles—they can also be services. Financial planning, medical checkups, and dry cleaning are all intangible interactions that do not result in ownership of an item, but rather provide a benefit to the client.[1] Products can also be experiences comprising specific memories or emotional attachments that occur in the mind of the consumer. Examples of these encounters might include eating at a gourmet restaurant, going to a concert, or visiting an amusement park; Disney World is more than a series of rides, or even just a vacation—it is an enchanting adventure.

The concept of selling the experience was pioneered by B. Joseph Pine and James Gilmore, who suggest a series of increasingly higher consumer expectations starting with commodities, goods, and services and ending with experiences and transformations.[2] Pine and Gilmore use coffee to illustrate this model. Coffee beans are available inexpensively as an everyday commodity; but once they are ground, flavored, packaged, and sold in a store, they become a good. Coffee served in a restaurant is slightly more expensive because of the brewing service. When ordering an espresso or cappuccino in a high-end coffeehouse, however, customers are buying the novelty, ambiance, and the theater of delivery. Pine and Gilmore state that consumers are willing to pay more for goods and services if they are packaged with entertainment, rituals, and atmosphere.

This same process applies to libraries. (See figure 4.1.) Let's say that a student needs an article for a class assignment. He can easily turn to the Web or browse the stacks for a publication that satisfies his basic need; at this level there is very little perceived difference between one article and another. However, he could also use a subject database designed to aid the search process and potentially find a more suitable article for the assignment. The student might also take advantage of reference services and talk with a librarian to learn about additional resources and search strategies. As the student applies this new knowledge and becomes immersed in the library, the encounter leads to a transformative feeling of accomplishment. In this context, providing instruction or research assistance is more than simply teaching students how to find material; rather, we provide them with motivation, guidance, confidence, and inspiration.

The library experience is a sequence of interactions set across a series of semesters: checking out a book, logging on to computers, studying for midterms, and cramming for finals. From a marketing standpoint, our objective is to identify and isolate opportune times to engage students by presenting different aspects of the library. In this way, the various components, such as books, databases, printing, or group study rooms, all become unique products. Each item can be promoted independently, but by strategically bundling items together, we can focus on serving specific needs at specific times, increasing awareness, and ultimately making the library more relevant to users. However, before we showcase our goods and services, we must first know what we have to offer.

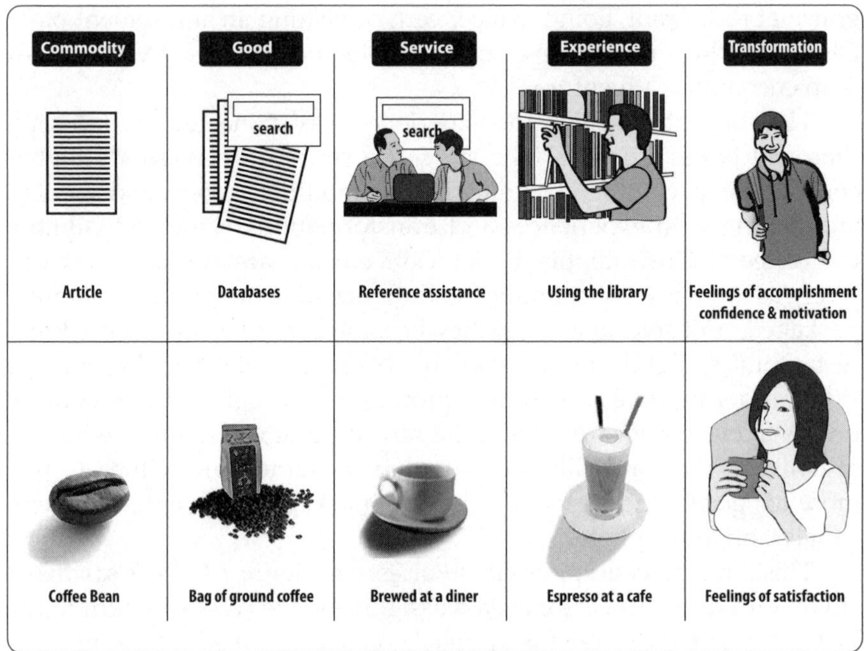

FIGURE 4.1
Library as product, experiential model

BUILDING YOUR PRODUCT INVENTORY

The product inventory is your conceptual warehouse; it is the mix of everything that users might encounter. Using a sheet of paper, copy the categories in table 4.1, listing all of the resources and services that your library provides. Don't worry about duplications or placing them in any order. Think broadly and try to record as many entries as possible.

Resources

The most identifiable item that a library offers is its collection; books and periodicals are our bread and butter. Ask anyone to describe a library and they will undoubtedly mention the large stacks of books or the piles of journals and old newspapers and magazines. Of course we offer many more specialized resources including financial information,

TABLE 4.1
Library Product Inventory Sheet

LIBRARY PRODUCT INVENTORY				
Resources	**Equipment**	**Space**	**Support**	**Experiences**

government documents, and technical reports, as well as multimedia collections containing CDs, DVDs, and software. However, most users never fully comprehend the size and scale of what is available to them. Or at least it's not the first thing that comes to mind.

Equipment

Most academic libraries offer a wide range of equipment and supplies. Think about all of the tangible objects that can be found in the building other than collections, from furniture and computers to printers, scanners, and photocopiers. Technology plays a large role in higher education, and libraries serve this need by offering rentals of laptops, cameras, digital voice recorders, camcorders, and other multimedia equipment. Some items also commonly available for sale are blank CDs, index cards, and various copy supplies.

Space

Space is another feature that libraries have to offer. While the emphasis in the past may have been on individual study, collaborative workspaces have become increasingly more prominent. Large computer labs, cafés, and comfortable seating areas are also becoming widespread characteristics of academic libraries. Along with these spaces, students might find museums, galleries, displays, and theaters or presentation stages. Aside from the physical library, you should also consider the virtual environment. With so much of our information and transactions occurring online, your digital real estate is a key location for the delivery of service and for awareness of products. This includes your website, course management system, online campus calendars, and social sites.

Support

The reference desk is an iconic symbol and perhaps the most defining service attribute of the library. However, there are many other valuable support touch points: Circulation handles user accounts, grants privileges, and issues materials; Interlibrary Loan ensures that documents are delivered; Systems makes sure that the computers stay online. Many academic libraries have also developed campus partnerships, expanding services to include assistance with tutoring, writing, advising, and counseling. Libraries have more to offer now than just research help; we have a full range of academic support services.

Experiences

While the other categories may be familiar to you, the concept of experiences is perhaps more abstract. This label pertains to personal emotions and memories associated with using the library. At a primal level, imagine the feelings of your students while they use all the different portions of your library. Building on the earlier example, a student may feel *stressed* about an assignment and consequently *frustrated* by his initial attempt to locate an article. After being *disappointed* with the process, the student *apprehensively* approaches the reference desk to get help. After receiving guidance, the student feels *confident* using a database and hence is *motivated* to complete the assignment. Afterward, he feels a *sense of accomplishment* from having learned how the library works.

Another way of understanding the experience concept is by examining what users are doing. Generate a list of verbs describing user actions, such as learning, teaching, talking, studying, watching, and creating; these activities should match up with specific library products. By viewing each library interaction as an engagement opportunity, librarians can leverage these encounters and ensure that users gain exposure to the full range of products that we make available.

Table 4.2 provides a sample inventory.

ASSEMBLING PRODUCT LINES

Once your inventory is complete, the next step is to assemble product lines. This process combines closely related items based on function. For example, Ralph Lauren sells premium lifestyle products in areas such as apparel, fragrances, and home furnishings. These broad categories also include several distinct clothing labels such as Polo Ralph Lauren, Big & Tall, RL Classics, Black Label, and Pink Pony. While Ralph Lauren includes a wide inventory, clothing is just one product line. Using this strategy, academic libraries also offer a distinct range of product lines:

Assistance: all of the various forms of help that are available to users

Access: privileges for obtaining print and online resources

Tools: resources, equipment, and supplies

Work areas: active spaces designed for productivity and collaboration

Study areas: quiet spaces designed for reading and contemplation

TABLE 4.2
Library Product Inventory Sheet—Sample

LIBRARY PRODUCT INVENTORY				
Resources	**Equipment**	**Space**	**Support**	**Experiences**
Archives	Audio Equipment	Auditorium	Advising	Accomplishment
Books	Binding	Bathrooms	Circulation Desk	Comfortable
CDs	Cameras	Café	Classes	Cramming
Conference Papers	Computers	Classroom	Computer Help	Creation
Databases	Copy Center	Displays (walls)	Course Mgt	Discovery
Dissertations	DVD/VHS Players	Elevators	Directions	Distraction
DVDs	Ethernet Cords	Enclosed Rooms	E-mail Help	Entertainment
E-books	Fax	Entranceway	Group Help	Epiphany
Govt Docs	Furniture	Exterior	IM Help	Escapism
Institutional Repository	Guest Computers	Group Areas	Interlibrary Loan	Exploration
Leisure Reading	Headphones	Help Desks	Media Help	Focus
Magazines	Lamination	Home Page	One-on-One Help	Frustration
Maps	Laptops	Museum	Online Tutorials	Inspiration
Micro-format	Micro-readers	Natural Light	Phone Help	Learning
Newspapers	Photocopiers	Parking Lot	Reference Desk	Quick Stop
Online Journals	Printing	Populated Areas	Security Desk	Relaxing
Print Journals	Projectors	Quiet Space	Shuttles	Serendipitous
Reference Books	Scanners	Reading Room	Subject Guides	Sharing
Special Collections	Software	Rehearsal Space	TA Help	Sleepy
Technical Reports	Supplies	Special Collections	Website/FAQ	Socializing
VHS	Televisions	Stacks	Workshops	Stressed
Video Games	Transparencies	Staff-Only Areas	Writing	Success
	Typewriters	Stage Area		Teaching
	Video Cameras	Stairs		Working Alone
	Whiteboards	Storage/Supplies		Working Collaboratively
	Wireless Access	Study Carrels		
		Utilities		
		Web Space		

Cultural encounters: intellectual and artistic features

Leisure: entertainment, social, and relaxing features

Let's look at how the product line scheme works. In our previous example of a student needing help, the focus was on finding material. However, perhaps the student later needed help editing his paper or designing a video or a website to supplement the presentation of his research. These are threads of academic support that reach beyond the typical transactions at the reference desk, yet may be available elsewhere in the library or through a campus partnership. By developing an *assistance* product line, libraries can promote the combination of all forms of help that are available, generating a much wider appeal. Help with research. Help with e-mail, passwords, or wireless connectivity. Help with media design. Help with algebra. The product line transforms the library from a place to do research into an epicenter of academic support.

Another product line, work areas, groups together all of the productivity and collaboration zones in your library. These are spaces for individuals as well as groups; places both with noise and without; computer stations as well as open tables; and other areas designed for comfort, instruction, or presentation rehearsal. The work areas product line showcases a variety of places, emphasizing the different functions of each zone that may be required at different times throughout the work cycle.

With your library product inventory list in front of you, use another blank sheet of paper to list the seven library product lines: assistance, access, tools, work areas, study areas, cultural encounters, and leisure. Try to fit each item from your inventory into at least one of the product line categories. (See table 4.3.) Don't worry about duplication.

Once your product lines are in place, try grouping associated items together as shown in table 4.4. For example, reference assistance may be obtained through various channels including in person, online chat, phone, or e-mail. Likewise, the leisure product line might include multiple formats such as DVDs, CDs, popular fiction, and magazines. Just as we use a classification system to place books together by their subject, we also want to group our products together to make it easier for us to communicate them collectively. Instead of just promoting reference, we can highlight all the various types of assistance and support available through the library.

You may discover other product lines that you want to highlight. These could be tailored for different audiences, such as faculty, staff

TABLE 4.3

Library Product Lines Sheet

LIBRARY PRODUCT LINES						
Assistance	Access	Tools	Work Areas	Study Areas	Culture	Leisure

TABLE 4.4
Library Product Lines Sheet—Sample

LIBRARY PRODUCT LINES						
Assistance	**Access**	**Tools**	**Work Areas**	**Study Areas**	**Culture**	**Leisure**
Reference In-person IM/Chat E-mail Phone Multimedia Writing Advising Tutoring Peer	Books Print Online Periodicals Print Online Technical reports Web	Printing Photocopying Binding Cameras Computers Scanners Software	Group areas Personal space Computer lab Tables Rooms Quiet areas Noisy areas	Quiet areas Noisy areas Reading room Carrels Café Group areas	Displays Exhibits Art Café DVDs Literature Events Space for clubs Speakers	Materials DVDs CDs Books Magazines Space Events Clubs Relaxation Café

members, researchers, alumni, or potential donors. As you begin thinking about all of the items that intersect with a particular population, group them together. For example, faculty product lines may feature Instruction Services, a collection of the classroom support services offered by the library, including face-to-face, one-on-one, web-based, video tutorials, or other methods. A Scholarly Communications product line could feature your institutional repository, copyright support, and other publishing-related services that your library offers. The objective is to capture and connect all similar products.

DESIGNING PRODUCT PORTFOLIOS

While the inventory represents everything that the library has to offer, and product lines serve as functional groupings, product portfolios are the strategic bundling of resources arranged to be of interest to specific user segments. This coordination enables us to package library products based on the anticipated needs and identities of our users. Nike exemplifies this marketing method; not only do they offer a wide array of athletic apparel and equipment, but they also bundle their products based on the sport. For example, a golfer can wear Nike footwear, as well as a variety of Nike shirts, pants, and hats, swing Nike golf clubs, and use Nike golf balls and other accessories. Nike promotes the athletic lifestyle, and by using their products a person indicates their dedication to the sport. Nike also markets products for all levels of expertise, from novice through professional; as an athlete moves deeper into the sport, Nike is there to fill their more sophisticated needs. Thereby, Nike provides a complete experience in the form of all of the equipment necessary to play golf, along with compelling slogans designed to inspire the consumer to strive toward athletic excellence.[3]

Let's look at how this method can be applied to an academic library. A student comes in to speak with a librarian (assistance) and is able to find a few journal articles (access). He sits down to read them (study area) and then makes a few photocopies (tools). Later in a computer commons (work area), he begins writing his paper and then grabs lunch in the café while talking with a friend (leisure). On his way out he notices a poster for an independent film series in the auditorium and decides to check it out (culture). This example, although somewhat simplistic, demonstrates how a single trip to the library uses a wide variety of our products and touches all seven of the product lines. While in this instance usage was happenstance, we can blend these products together to create richer library experiences.

The advantage of designing portfolios lies in the ability to package library products in a way that maximizes appeal to select user groups. (See figure 4.2.) Computer science majors will be interested in online programming books (access), design software (tools), hands-on workshops (assistance), and the multimedia lab (work area). Incoming freshmen may be interested in the library commons (work area) so that they can use computers (tools) to check e-mail and print assignments; they may also seek quiet spaces to review class notes (study area) and peruse popular magazines and DVDs (leisure). Biology majors might need to use online course reserves (access), meet with their teaching assistant (assistance), practice for a group presentation (work area), and prepare for a test (study areas). Environmentally active students may want to read books and government reports on ecology (access), create or view public displays (culture), and use rooms (work space) for club meetings.

As we move forward to designing messages, we can craft unique product portfolios that match specific user groups. What items would be of most interest to each major? Don't think only about resources, but also about spaces and the types of assistance that they might require depending on their curriculum. For example, in working with the School of Mechanical Engineering, I know exactly when students will need to

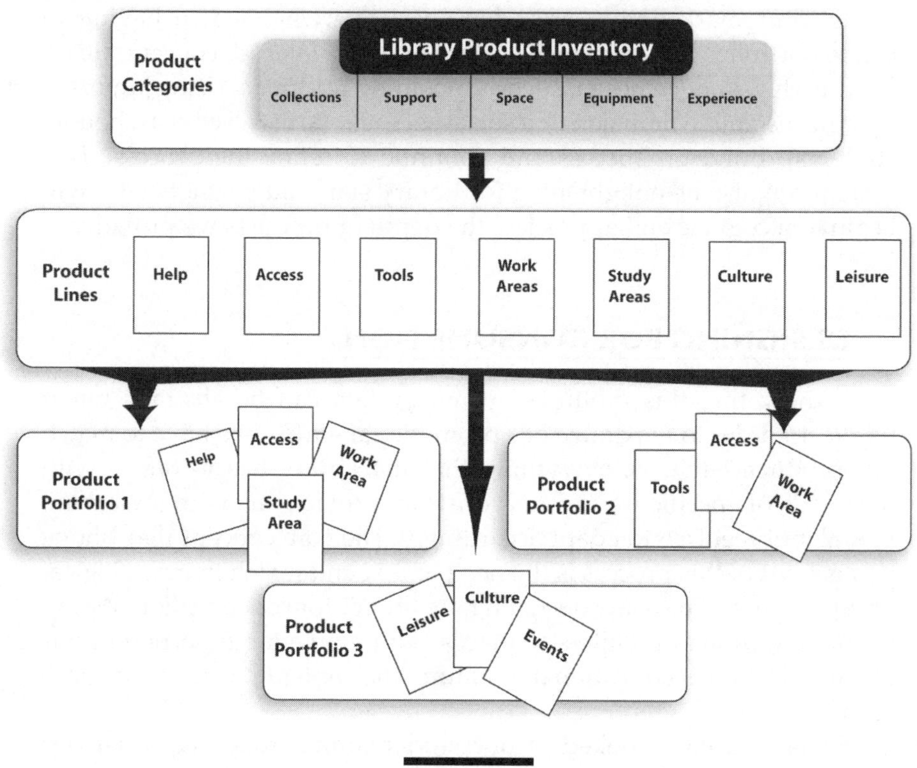

FIGURE 4.2
Library as product flowchart

learn about patent research, use technical data, and search scientific literature. I know when they will need to use specific software programs, prepare a presentation, and study for tests. Having helped hundreds of undergraduates in this discipline, I can also anticipate the common problems they will encounter, when they will face these difficulties, and how I can most effectively assist them.

While of course each student uses the library differently, and we can't attempt to construct a customized product portfolio for every one, this approach does provide a framework for organizing communication. Subject librarians may find it beneficial to assemble portfolios for the disciplines they cover. If nothing else, it will help to intellectualize every point of contact that their students typically encounter within the library.

In your marketing efforts, don't feel overwhelmed in having to create portfolios for every niche group of users. Instead, concentrate on a few each year or semester, such as incoming freshmen, rising juniors, a specific discipline or major, or a social segment (artists, activists, honors students). Build on success and continue to refine the process. This system can also be enlightening for library staff and partners who will begin to recognize and appreciate the depth of products we provide.

DESIGNING FOR CONSUMPTION

I know that this multiple-layered system can be abstract, but it works. In order to maximize our promotional efforts, we have to match our products—that is, everything that the library has to offer—with the needs of specific users. This construct provides us with a working model, but feel free to adapt accordingly. The core concept that I hope you get out of this process is the need to mix and match items in logical groups. In essence we are designing the library for consumption. We are breaking it down into bite-size pieces. Although a large portion of our communication is educational in nature, the content has to make sense to the user.

So far we have looked at our students and examined what our libraries have to offer them. The next step is figuring out their perceptions, preferences, motivations, misinformation, gaps of information, and the how, why, and what they use within the library. It's time to do some research.

NOTES

1. Philip Kotler, *Principles of Marketing* (Upper Saddle River, NJ: Prentice Hall, 2001).
2. B. Joseph Pine and James Gilmore, *The Experience Economy: Work Is Theater and Every Business a Stage* (Boston: Harvard Business School Press, 1999).
3. Robert Goldman and Stephen Papson, *Nike Culture: The Sign of the Swoosh* (Thousand Oaks, CA: Sage Publications, 1998).

5 Conducting Marketing Research

Imagine that you are appointed to your library's marketing committee and that the budget for the upcoming year is $5,000. How do you spend the money? How do you decide what posters to print, what events to host, or what services to promote? Do you continue doing what's always been done or try something new? Members of your marketing committee will probably have a lot of creative ideas, but ultimately you are working with limited time and a set budget. Therefore, before the committee can even begin planning for promotional activities, you need to find out what users need to know, what they value, and the best way to communicate with them. Welcome to the world of marketing research. While designing an advertising campaign is fun, assessment should always be the first step of your promotional effort.

ASKING THE RIGHT QUESTIONS

The purpose of doing any type of research is to solve a problem; marketing research is no different. It is a learning process, a journey along a serendipitous path filled with many detours. You definitely want a plan in place—otherwise you'll get lost along the way—yet it is OK to get sidetracked occasionally and to explore an unexpected route.

Everything begins with a question. How do we get more students in the library? How can we increase reference interactions? What's the best way to tell people about a new database? How should we promote this event? I view each of these as a communication puzzle. This doesn't necessarily mean that something is wrong or needs to be fixed; instead, I see it as a challenge that can be worked out logically. Marketing research provides a loosely interconnected framework that we can apply to find potential answers to our questions. What we are really hunting for are solutions.

There are many useful techniques for conducting marketing research, but as famed statistician Edward Tufte warns, research should not be method-driven.[1] Instead of always relying on a survey, we need to select the best methods for what we need to know. We need to consider all the possible questions, define the issue, and then find techniques that are appropriate to obtain the necessary information.

Let's take a look at the reference desk as an example. Say that over the last two semesters the number of questions asked by students has steadily declined. The common approach is to ask, how can we increase traffic? The department then conducts a survey and finds out that many students do not know about the research help service. This then is a problem of awareness. In response, the department develops a campaign to get the word out about librarians. They plaster the campus with posters, pens, and fliers and then wait for the questions to start rolling in.

While there is nothing wrong with this strategy (in fact, mass exposure is the preferred method of many Fortune 500 companies), it fails to dig deeply into the matter. Another approach would be to consider asking, why are the numbers so low? This becomes a core question that we can study. Is there a lack of awareness or a lack of need? Have assignments changed? What is different about the way that students conduct research or write papers? Are there additional channels that librarians could use to interact with users? What motivates students to seek reference assistance, and how do they feel about approaching the desk? Are telephone, e-mail, and chat numbers declining as well? Are users satisfied with the customer service and the quality of assistance that they receive? How did they find out about it? Why don't some students use the library at all?

These types of questions aspire to paint the big picture. We can use marketing research to probe deeper in the student psyche by attempting to understand why a person needs assistance in the first place, the reason that she chose to approach the reference desk, whether the encounter was worth her time, the likelihood that she would return again, and what she might tell others about the experience. Gaining insight into these distinctions not only enables us to improve our service, but also strengthens the way that we promote reference.

It is important early on for library staff to brainstorm as many questions as possible. While it is easy, and perhaps natural, for us to focus on ourselves (how can we increase our numbers?), we have to push self-interest aside and focus on our users (why do they need this product?). Instead of just concocting ways of getting students to use a database or to attend an event, we should delve into the question of *why*. Why should they use whatever it is that we have to offer? Why should they care? What is the benefit? Which of their needs is being fulfilled? Once we start asking these types of questions, we gain insight into the emotional and functional attributes that drive usage. After this we can begin defining the target audience, designing a meaningful and motivating message, and selecting the best delivery method. But let's not get ahead of ourselves. There is a wide array of research methods that we can use to tackle these deep questions. Here is a peek into the marketer's toolbox.

MARKETING RESEARCH TECHNIQUES

I highly recommend using a mixed methods approach to marketing research, combining a variety of techniques in order to develop the full story that you are studying. The primary objective with marketing research is to uncover your users' perceptions: their thoughts, reactions, problems, preferences, and experiences. The following methods are the most commonly used by market researchers: data, surveys, personal interviews, secret shoppers, follow-up inquiries, comment cards, polling, focus groups, and ethnographic techniques. Let's look at each of them.

Data

Most academic libraries keep stockpiles of statistics. For the marketing researcher this is a window into the character of the library. Data will often provide hints or fragments of the story that you are trying to unravel, but they can't tell you everything. Let's say for example that your gate count rises significantly. Why? Did professors assign more research papers? Did the library add more computers? Is there a new café?

Data are useful in finding correlations with the behavior of your users. Always look for the meaning behind the numbers. For example, when I first look at a set of statistics, I seek out anything unusual: the highs and lows and the anomalies—anything that doesn't fit. This helps to define the scope of the problem. Next I look for any patterns. Are there particular times when services are very busy? Are there times when they are not busy at all? Is usage consistent throughout the semester? The objective should always be to translate the data into a narrative statement; interpret them so that an outsider can understand the significance without seeing the numbers. *Juniors spend more time in the library than any other user group. Students using the library in the evening stay for an average of three hours.*

You can also use data to identify new advertising opportunities. The Georgia Tech Library has a rehearsal studio that students can use to practice group presentations. When a student signs up to reserve this space, the library collects their course information. (See figure 5.1.) These data reveal that a wide variety of classes use this space. As we start to put the story together, several questions come to mind. How do students find out about the rehearsal studio? How far in advance do they reserve it? Where do they go if the room is already booked? Why do so many biology students reserve the space? Why are there so few humanities or social science users?

These data show the wide spectrum of classes that require presentations. While some classes are heavy users of the space, many are not.

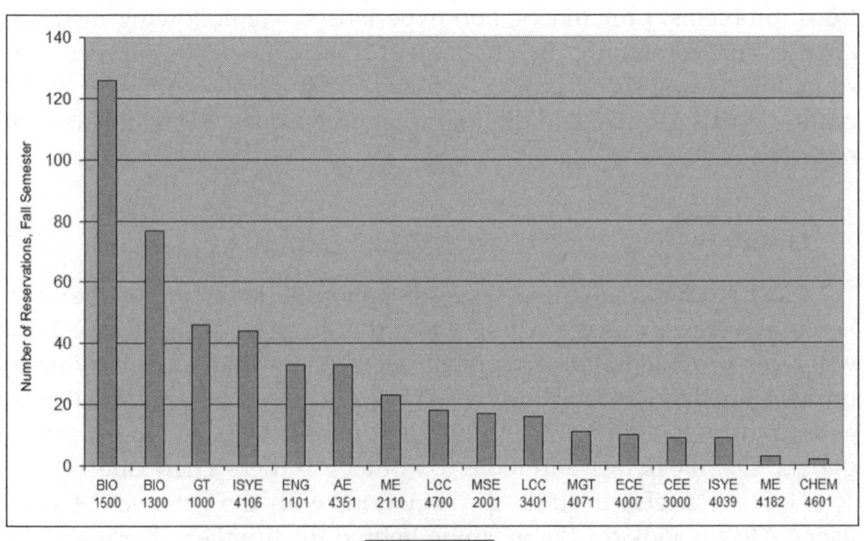

FIGURE 5.1

Presentation rehearsal room reservations, sample data

We can see that some courses, such as ME 4182 and CHEM 4601, are minimal users, suggesting perhaps that those students might be better able to take advantage of the rehearsal space. This finding signifies which classes are *underperforming* and could be candidates for promotional initiatives. Maybe those students are unfamiliar with the library's rehearsal space. By focusing on the courses that we know require group presentations, we are able to reach students with a particular need, increasing the chances that our message will be on target. Simply put, we promote the rehearsal studio specifically to students with presentation assignments.

Data are also valuable for assessing the impact of your promotional activities. Chapter 10 focuses on evaluating advertising efforts, but as a rule of thumb keep in mind that marketing should be clearly focused on generating results; you want the audience to react in some manner to the message you produce. Your existing data can serve as a baseline, a controlled measurement or snapshot of current usage. These numbers can later be reexamined after an advertising campaign launches to see if the promotion worked. In short, data can help us *prove* that advertising had an impact. There are all types of numbers that libraries can collect; use them to tell a story. Data are an excellent starting point but should not be our sole metric.

Surveys

Surveys are the most common tool for marketing research. They can be created quickly, are easy to administer, and constitute a minimal cost. The Web has dramatically increased the spread and application of surveys; in fact, it has created a danger of survey fatigue. Studies suggest that college students are constantly bombarded with surveys from the various clubs, departments, and organizations on campus and that because of this, response rates have declined.[2] Keep this in mind when you are planning a survey. Although you may have good intentions, users may not always be willing to participate or give your survey their full attention.

The objective of any survey is to collect a representative response to a series of questions. This is a formal and standardized process of finding out what the majority of your users think. By sampling a portion of your total population, you are able to form a generalized opinion. *Basic Research Methods for Librarians* provides a helpful table to determine your ideal sample size.[3] For example, if your total student population is 10,000, then your sample should be 370. Response rate is another key component and will vary depending on format. A good rule of thumb is that a 25 percent return offers a high degree of reliability. So if you send your survey to 370 students, you would hope that 93 of them respond.

Because using the sampling method allows for more confidence in your results, it is very common, although less effective, for libraries to place questionnaires on their website or out in public spaces. Although this strategy will generate results, the data are less reliable. In these cases, participants are self-selected and may have a personal agenda to promote. Additionally, this method requires that students are either in the building or visiting your website and happen upon your questionnaire at a time that is convenient for them. While these so-called open surveys may not be as accurate or representative, they can be useful for gaining a quick impression—and sometimes that's all you need.

Surveys come in many shapes and sizes, and questions typically fall into three category types: multiple choice, open-ended, and ratings scales. These formats allow for a tremendous amount of versatility, enabling you to measure attitudes, values, perceptions, beliefs, desires, and past behaviors.[4] While web-based questionnaires have emerged as the predominate format, surveys can also be administered in person, over the phone, and on paper. These forms typically result in higher return rates, but they require more time and effort on the part of the library staff.

While surveys are an efficient tool for measuring a large population, they have some drawbacks. Sometimes the problem lies with the questions themselves, which can be leading (*Is the library the best place to study?*) or biased (*What makes the library the best place to study?*). One of the dangers of surveys, or of any assessment tool, is that the researcher already has ideas in mind and is simply looking for users to confirm those notions. Be sure that students are not simply telling you what you want to hear. Aside from the questionnaire, the respondents themselves can inject bias. Surveys tend to attract participants with strong opinions, both positive and negative, which can skew your results. Additionally, participants may rush through the questionnaire or haphazardly fill in their answers. This is especially true if they are only interested in an offered incentive. Surveys depend on the subjects' motivation, honesty, memory, and ability to respond. Some participants might be unable to provide a reasonable answer, particularly if they are unfamiliar with the subject being asked, and consequently they might guess at a possible answer. Another downside is that there is typically no intervention available for probing or further explanation. Despite these limitations, surveys can be insightful and an excellent way to take the pulse of your user population. Just be sure to check results against other research methods to ensure consistency.

Personal Interviews

Personal or in-depth interviews are another way to initiate exploratory research. These sessions tap into the knowledge and opinions of expert users. In fact, anyone associated with your research topic is a potential candidate for an interview: current students, alumni, faculty, library employees, or librarians at other institutions. Participants should be selected based on their ability to provide useful information; it is also important to include individuals with differing points of view.

Let's say that you want to better understand how students use your group study space. After identifying individuals who are regular users of this area, approach them to find out their perceptions. What characteristics do they like or dislike? Why do they prefer that location? What are their thoughts on the atmosphere, aesthetics, and furniture? How might the area be improved? Next, approach students who are studying together in other places on campus. Ask them similar questions about the space that they are using. By comparing the responses of these two perspectives, you might find elements that are missing, opportunities for improving, or better ways to define library space. You might also discover a lack of awareness about group work areas in the library.

When you are conducting these interviews, avoid using a formal questionnaire. Instead, give respondents the freedom to choose which topics are discussed. Although it is advisable to have a few major points written down to help guide the session, don't be too prescriptive. Using the example above, let your interviewees bring up subjects, such as lighting, electrical outlets, noise, or cushioned seating, at their own pace. Your objective is to get each respondent to share as much information as possible. I have found that talking with people individually works best, because it encourages them to be more forthcoming. Additionally, these interviews should be informal, so a casual setting like a café or the student center can help the participant relax. I typically schedule each session for one hour and offer each subject a beverage and light snack. Furthermore, you might also include a library walk-through with the participant. Sometimes when someone encounters the space, it spurs further insights or memories.

Due to the hectic nature of students' lives, it can be difficult to get them to commit time to face-to-face interviews. As a substitute, you can e-mail individuals several short questions. I recommend asking no more than three questions, and be sure that they are open-ended, such as, how do you typically use the library? What are some ways that we can improve the space? What do you wish you had known about the library as an incoming freshman? This method of correspondence also opens channels for further dialogue and additional follow-up questions.

Whether in person, or via instant messenger or e-mail, talking with people who are familiar with your specific research area will enable you to formulate initial impressions. Their insights will help you further define the issues and establish your research scope. While much of the material you collect from these interviews will be anecdotal, it provides a foundation for the rest of your investigation.

Secret Shoppers

The secret shopper technique is a good method to use at the start of each fall semester. Ask several freshmen to approach any service point, seeking help with finding a book on any topic of their personal interest. Ask them to enter the library with their topic in mind and to leave with a book or article in hand. Afterward, have them map out their journey and write a brief description about the transactions, sharing the details of their encounter. The focus of this exercise is not necessarily the quality of customer service—unless the student remarks on a bad experience—but instead reveals all the steps that novice users take to complete the task. How does this shape their perception about using the library? Is it easy or difficult? Do they get lost? What questions did they have along the way? By looking for common difficulties or frustrations, we can attempt to remove barriers and look for better ways to improve signage and communications.

Secret shoppers are useful for measuring the quality of customer service; they can also serve to uncover communication problems. By comparing a handful of such interactions, you can discover problems, unfilled needs, or areas that need to be expanded or better explained. Of course you might find examples of exemplary service, too. The benefit of using the secret shopper method is that frontline staff are unaware that they are being evaluated and therefore interact with the subject in a natural manner. However, I recommend informing staff that this form of evaluation might be used periodically to gauge customer service. Emphasize that they are not being judged or critiqued personally, but that the secret shopper technique is used occasionally throughout the year as a means of assessing the customer experience.

Follow-up Inquiries

Following up with customers after they make a purchase is a common technique that businesses use as a measure of quality assurance. If you buy a new car, you'll likely hear from representatives inquiring about the process. This allows companies to keep tabs on customer satisfaction and to pinpoint areas in the purchasing cycle that could be improved. Librarians can also benefit from this method. Each semester I randomly select ten students who have reserved the library's presentation rehearsal space and e-mail them a short series of questions, such as how they found out about the room, what equipment they used, and how their eventual presentation turned out in the end.

Consider all the different products that your library offers: space, equipment, resources, and academic support services. Each of these elements presents feedback opportunities, a chance to collect descriptive evidence revealing a story of usage. As you plan your marketing research, consider options for contacting users of specific items and conducting a follow-up interview or short e-mail survey. If possible, try building this type of assessment into all library services. You do not need a large pool of respondents; six or seven individuals each semester is enough.

I have found that students are generally grateful to be asked to participate, and most are willing to spend a few minutes providing their input. While you may consider administering these questionnaires at the point of return (i.e., returning books, returning a laptop, returning a key to a study room), I have found that students are more reflective several days or even weeks afterward. Regardless of when you conduct these exit interviews, hearing back from users about specific services is informative.

Of course privacy is another issue; you want to be sure that you are not compromising the identity of your students, so be sure that they are randomly chosen and that their names are stripped away from comments that are shared with staff.

Comment Cards

Tell us what you think! Many companies use comment cards as a way to solicit feedback. These forms are everywhere, from hospitals and hotels to restaurants, mechanics, and retail outlets. Managers want to know what customers think, particularly about problems they encounter, enabling companies to address unsatisfying experiences. If the respondent leaves contact information, the manager can try to clarify any misconceptions and alleviate the grievance. While this method tends to attract extreme opinions, both positive and negative, providing a direct communication channel with users is a valuable assessment tool. Starbucks takes their customers' feedback very seriously, and it has led to many improvements, such as the inclusion of low-fat milk and the development of Frappuccinos.[5]

Libraries can also benefit from this opportunity to gather insights. Traditional comment cards can be placed near service desks or the entryway; additionally, flip charts seeking user input can periodically be distributed throughout the library. Online forms, though, are the best method for gathering opinions. In my experience, students and faculty tend to use feedback forms similarly to a reference e-mail service, describing their frustrations with using databases or obtaining material. However, users also provide a wide range of views, such as collection recommendations, suggestions for guest speakers or events, experiences with customer service, and commentary on the building's temperature. The strategic approach for libraries is to address each comment personally, as well as removing all personal information and posting it online. This allows others to see answers or solutions to common problems and puts a positive spin on the library as a responsive organization.

Polling

Polling is a quick way to gather instant feedback. Although results may not be generalizable, polling students for their opinions is helpful. When developing a poll, keep it brief and avoid open-ended inquiries that require a long response. I recommend asking no more than two or three questions and have found that yes or no, multiple choice, rating scales, and short answers work best. You also don't want to make the questions too overwhelming, confusing, or discouraging for participants. Inexpensive food and drink items also make good incentives.

Polling is particularly valuable throughout planning stages because you can quickly gather numerous impressions. For example, if you are launching a new library website, you could show prototype layouts to students to gauge their preferences. Negative responses could alert you to potential problems early in the process, preventing major redesign work later on. Additionally, you could use polling for branding or satisfaction questions, asking participants to rate library services on a scale of one to ten or to note the first thing that comes to mind when they think of the library or specific library products.

Facebook, the popular online social network, offers a convenient polling feature that allows you to address a multiple-choice question to your entire community. The cost is $0.25 per response, and the participants are randomly selected; results are typically delivered within twenty-four hours. (See figure 5.2.)

While online polling has the advantage of quickly gathering results from a large sample, in-person methods invite richer data collection. Walking around the library or the campus provides a direct connection between you and the user, and this interpersonal contact can lead to follow-up questions and extensive feedback. It also demonstrates that the library staff are interested in student opinions.

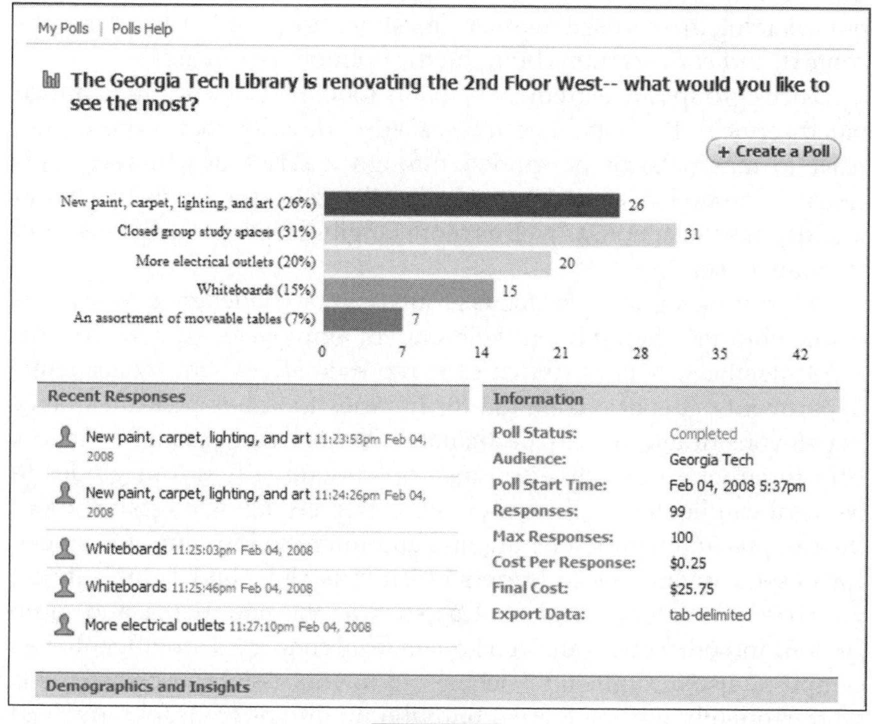

FIGURE 5.2
Facebook poll

During a renovation research project I used polling to test results that surfaced during interviews, observations, and focus groups. I wanted to see how a wide range of students would respond to the various recommendations that were gathered through other research methods. I decided to poll several different user segments, such as students working in groups, students who are regularly in the library, and students completely unfamiliar with library services. Respondents provided a vast scope of reactions that were helpful in finalizing our design. Polling is quick and easy and can greatly supplement other assessment efforts.

Focus Groups

Focus groups are another tool synonymous with marketing research. Tucked away in office parks across the nation, these moderated discussions are used by Fortune 500 companies to find out what people think. Focus groups are precisely that—individuals brought together to share their attitudes about products, services, concepts, advertisements, ideas, or packaging in a focused manner. Questions are posed in an interactive context, and conversations build on the opinions of others.

Focus groups are extremely valuable for exploring current or anticipated services. Participants can be asked to describe their experiences, react to materials, or be guided through a series of activities. This research method is useful for measuring theoretical concepts like brand identity or satisfaction, as well as more tangible aspects, such as use and usability of services.

Recruiting students for focus groups can be challenging. Many academic libraries often rely on their student employees, student government members, honors students, or representatives sent by academic departments. It is also common for libraries to issue open calls, inviting anyone interested to participate. Besides these usual suspects, I try to target a more diverse range of students. I find tour guides to be ideal candidates because they are extremely knowledgeable about the campus and tend to be outgoing and interested in campus matters. I also send invitations to leaders of campus clubs and organizations, members of student media groups such as the newspaper and radio station, and others who are well known, well connected, or influential on campus. I also recommend reaching out to your regular users: students who frequently use the library, but who might not be deeply involved with campus activities. They often have a lot to share, but you have to ask. When recruiting for focus groups, you should aim to have a diverse mix of attendees, across age, discipline, and experience levels using library services, unless you intend to study a specialized audience, such as females, international students, sophomores, or business majors. One of the strategies that I have learned in recruiting is to encourage participants to bring a friend, which increases the likelihood that they will attend, makes them feel comfortable socially, and also increases your turnout.

The ideal size for a focus group is seven to twelve participants, with a typical session lasting for an hour and a half. I find later hours work best with student schedules; they are more likely to attend evening sessions. Pizza, of course, is always a good incentive. How many focus group sessions should you host? It depends. If your topic is broad or abstract, such as how students use or feel about the library, then you should probably hold at least ten sessions. However, if you are investigating something very specific, such as study room policies, printing, or library instruction, then four to six sessions are probably enough. The best indication that you've reached the end is when you hit a saturation point; this is when your sessions no longer yield any new information. If you start hearing the same responses over and over again, then you have probably uncovered all the major themes.

When it comes to crafting questions, Richard Krueger's *Developing Questions for Focus Groups* is the definitive guide.[6] Your objective as a moderator is to get people talking with each other instead of simply responding to you directly. The goal is to have a group conversation, rather than a group interview. Krueger suggests using *think back* questions (think back to a time when . . .), allowing participants to draw from their memories. He also encourages using open-ended questions that are sequenced to begin exploring the topic broadly and then narrowing as the questions move forward. Here is an example:

1. Tell me about some of the class assignments that you've completed in the past year or that you are working on this semester.
2. Walk me through the process of a research paper. I am interested in how you choose your topic, find information, and synthesize everything.
3. A few of you have mentioned using the library journals online. Let's talk about that. How does the library fit into your work flow? How have you used the library for assignments?
4. When you are working on these types of assignments, or when you are using the library, what are the biggest challenges?

5. Would you ever consider asking a librarian for help? Follow-up: What do you think would make these assignments easier? (Is it a motivation problem, are the databases confusing, are users finding too much or too little information?)

These questions start with the general topic of completing assignments and drill down to getting help. Instead of just asking students their opinions about reference assistance, I try to create a context. What I am really interested in are the pitfalls, stumbling blocks, critical moments, and motivators, which I can then embed into how I promote reference librarians.

When wrapping up a focus group session, Krueger recommends summarizing all the major themes that were discussed. This allows participants the opportunity to ensure that all the main points were covered correctly, to stress anything that is critical, and to clarify or add any additional details.

There is more to facilitating conversations than just posing questions to your students. Activities are a great way to stimulate discussion and to make sure that all group members have a chance to participate. I try to include a group exercise early in the session so that individuals feel comfortable and bond with one another. Activities are also helpful because they prompt a response and provide you with a tangible take-away or artifact, such as a drawing or a list. Students also typically enjoy the interactive and visual participation. Jean Bystedt has assembled an excellent collection of focus group activities.[7] Here are a few strategies that I use regularly:

Photos

Images are great for initiating conversation. What do participants notice? What stands out for them? I often use photos of the library as a backdrop to generate discussion: how do students use particular study space, what are their thoughts on table arrangements, what's missing, or what would they change? It is one thing to talk about a computer lab or the reference desk abstractly, but placing an image in front of them prompts a more concrete response. While conducting research for a renovation project, I displayed numerous photos of library spaces from around the country and asked students to describe and evaluate them. This activity enabled me to test their reactions to furniture, aesthetics, and layout. Pictures are worth a thousand words, so use them to discover the story of your users.

Projection

Projection is a useful technique for uncovering the brand or personality of your library. This exercise can be done individually or out loud as a group. Participants are asked to create a persona for your building, your services, or whatever it is that you want to study. This is how I might frame the question:

> Let's say that the library is a person. What does he or she like? Who does he or she resemble? What is his or her age and gender? What is his or her personality? How does the library interact with others? Who is he or she friends with?

Once they get started, students really get into this activity. I use this technique when consulting to obtain a broad perception of a library. In one case, students repeatedly described their library as a tired old man. He is dull and not well groomed. His clothes are tattered, stained, drab, and dark. This man is a quiet type, perhaps even a bit shy, and his friends are generally studious people. He is retired and his glory days are long gone. This description provides an enlightening look at how students perceived their library; it strongly indicates a need to update physical spaces, services, and the overall image of the library. While projection can be abstract, it allows users to think vividly and creatively about the library.

Targeting

This is another exercise that is a lot of fun and generates conversation. Focus group participants are given a sheet of paper with a shooting target printed on it, along with several multicolored sticky dots. Each dot corresponds with a question: blue might be customer service, green might be group study space, gold the overall perception of the library, and so on. The content and number of questions are customized to whatever you want to measure. The bull's-eye at the center of the target represents a high score, while each expanding ring indicates a lower value. After students have placed their dots on their target, invite volunteers to share their results and to explain their decision making. While they present their results, look for any glaring patterns; for example, did most participants place customer service near the bull's-eye or farther away? How does group space compare to individual space? How are collections perceived? Aside from their ratings, the real value is derived from the discussions that ensue.

Mind Map

Mind maps are similar to concept maps, which are often used when exploring a research topic. You begin with a broad theme like air transportation and then follow all the related subjects, such as security, safety, costs, fees, airports, luggage, air traffic control, and legislation. This process not only provides a global scope, but enables you to identify interconnected issues. You can apply this strategy to libraries as well. Give participants a blank sheet of paper and have them map out their library experience. This exercise could be framed around something specific, such as collections, or kept wide open. Participants could also be asked to map out how they complete an assignment or to illustrate their academic performance. The value of this activity is that it allows you to see the connections and familiarity with various library products. Similar to the targeting exercise, mind mapping is also valuable for starting conversation among the group.

Affinity Exercise

The affinity technique is helpful for generating a large number of ideas. It is a great tool for exploring a new research topic and gauging the scope of an issue. We use this method frequently at Georgia Tech, and we've provided a detailed guide online.[8] Here's how it works:

Each individual is issued a pen and a stack of sticky notes. The group is then given a topic or scenario and asked to respond out loud and in writing. Students might be asked to envision the library of their dreams and then to describe what they see as they walk through it. While an individual speaks, have that person commit each unique idea to a separate sticky note. These conversations will ebb and flow. Prompt the group from time to time by asking what services, furniture, or atmosphere they see in the space. How does it work and what else should there be? This process should last for about thirty minutes.

The next stage is to place all of the sticky notes on a wall. Participants will then work collectively to group their responses together and to create a label for each category. For example, "technology" might include desktop computers, laptops, wireless Internet, wired Internet, scanners, software, projectors, and power outlets. They should attempt to group all responses, placing any outliers aside.

The final step of the process is for the students to create a name for the overarching concept. This could be something like "the twenty-first-century library," "the ideal study space," or "everything we need to succeed." After all of their thoughts are grouped together, you can start engaging students about their ideas. This technique bundles the perceptions, preferences, and expectations of users into unified themes. Not only does it reveal areas that might be expanded or improved upon, but it provides insight into the direction that the library should be heading in order to be relevant to its users.

Focus groups bring us closer to the students' mindset; however, there is some question about whether librarians should be administering these sessions in the first place. Perhaps we are too invested and our bias may creep in. Watching other librarians moderate, I often notice a tendency to apologize for poor service and to use the sessions to promote collections, explain policies, or to educate students about the library. It is important that we remain neutral and inquisitive and try to distance any emotional attachment that we have. This can be developed through training, experience, and evaluation. In order to become better facilitators, it helps to receive feedback from a colleague who can observe us objectively. A problem I had was trying to dialogue too much after asking a question, rather than sitting back and allowing participants enough time to expound. Over time and with enough practice, I believe that librarians can become effective moderators.

When used in combination with other research methods, focus groups yield an enormous amount of information and offer a visceral glimpse of the library through the student's eyes. Of course these sessions will not provide all of the answers that you are seeking, but they do allow you to interact directly with your users. This type of exposure can aid our marketing objective of creating effective, meaningful, and targeted communication.

Ethnographic Techniques

A steady infusion of anthropology has been seeping into the world of marketing. Ethnography, which originated as the study of foreign cultures through immersion, has evolved into the seeking of an in-depth understanding of consumers. The emergence of these techniques takes research out of a controlled laboratory and places it into the homes, offices, stores, and natural environments of customers. Instead of asking someone how they feel about a product, marketers use this approach to observe people using the item and to note their successes, failures, and limitations.

Marketers use anthropology to perceive their customers' point of view, gaining insights into the language, myths, feelings, aspirations, and emotions behind purchasing behavior.[9] This cultural perceptiveness is ideal when little is known about a targeted user group or when new insights are necessary. For example, if the objective is to understand shopping patterns, the researcher can follow consumers through the process, focusing on the decision-making moments, which can then be used for future advertising.

The University of Rochester (New York) has done some inspiring work in applying ethnographic studies within the library setting.[10] The University of Rochester Libraries hired an anthropologist and treated their campus as a fieldwork experiment; they were able to improve library services and physical spaces based on their findings. The practice also served as a bonding experience for staff, who gained a deeper awareness of the student lifestyle and a stronger level of camaraderie. Here are some of the techniques that they used:

Mapping Diaries

What exactly do students do all day? To answer this question, Rochester librarians gave campus maps to several students and had them plot out their day. Obviously there were core destinations, such as dorm rooms, classes, and dining halls, but they could also see where the library, the gym, and leisure activities fit into the schedule. One of the most insightful discoveries from the maps was the on-the-go lifestyles of many of the students; they are constantly moving from one place to another. The study also revealed that students work on their assignments late in the evenings, and so the traditional nine-to-five reference mentality does not match the availability of students. This type of research is helpful because it puts library use into perspective and enables us to see students' lives more generally.

Design Workshops

Librarians recruited students and asked them to design their ideal library spaces. This could include furniture, services, and resources—whatever they felt was necessary. Out of these notes and sketches several themes emerged, including the need for flexible space, comfort, staff support, and technology and tools. While these elements helped to guide renovations, they could also be used in communication messages about the library to ensure that they are on target.

The next phase of the process included giving students paper cutouts of a wide variety of furniture and asking them to arrange the tables and chairs within the library's floor plan. This exercise was enlightening for the librarians and staff because they were able to talk with students about their decisions, and they found that their own opinions differed greatly from those of their users.

Photo Surveys

In an attempt to view the campus through the eyes of their students, library staff gave each participant a disposable camera and a list of twenty things to photograph. The list included "all the stuff you take to class," "your dorm," "your favorite place to study," and "a place in the library where you feel lost." After reviewing the images, library staff interviewed students about their photos. This allowed them to capture both visual and oral data, enriching their perspective. Instead of just asking questions as we do with surveys, polls, or focus groups, this activity opened the door for personal reflection and informed investigation. Rochester staff found that students were excited by this task and very open to sharing their lives.

Interviews

The Rochester team, aided by a library student assistant and an anthropology graduate student, journeyed around campus to interview students actively working on research papers. They aimed to find out how students felt about their assignments and the methods they were using to complete them. One of the pivotal discoveries was that librarians were almost never considered when students needed research help. Furthermore, students associated librarians with books and print material. This discovery cries out for an advertising campaign informing students about the role of librarians and the resources we make available.

One breakthrough in their research was that many students spoke regularly with their parents about papers and other assignments. The library staff addressed this insight by hosting a parents' brunch during orientation, in which their motto was "every class has a librarian." If they could get this message across to parents, then perhaps the information would be passed along to the students. This exemplifies the value that libraries can gain from conducting marketing research.

Many more activities were performed by the Rochester staff; I highly recommend reading about their anthropological adventure. Whether you develop an extensive program or just dabble with a few of these techniques, the act of studying, observing, and understanding the actions and preferences of our students can vastly improve the manner and effectiveness in which we communicate with them.

LibQUAL+

LibQUAL+ is a customer service survey administered by the Association of Research Libraries (ARL). This instrument was derived from ServQUAL, one of the major tools used by the marketing industry to evaluate the expectation and delivery of commercial services. The LibQUAL+ instrument measures three thematic areas: the Library as Place, Information Control, and the Effect of Service. This tool allows you to obtain a broad view of your users' perceptions, desires, and expectations. I like to think of it as a library's report card.

In addition to numerous questions, LibQUAL+ features a comment box inviting participants to express opinions and make suggestions. These statements are valuable because respondents report issues of which managers may be unaware. For example, a college in Georgia was able to respond to comments about a pinhole-size crack in a windowpane that disturbed students on windy days. Another library used results to convince their campus administration to install additional lighting outside the library leading to a parking deck nearby.

Along with the qualitative and quantitative aspects, LibQUAL+ also provides the ability to benchmark results with other libraries. You can compare your data with peer or aspiration institutions and discover areas of excellence, as well as areas to focus on improving. The real benefit of LibQUAL+ is that it allows you to carve your data into various user segments, such as gender, year, discipline, and frequency of library use. This survey enables you to see if specific majors or user groups are comparatively satisfied with the library. (See figure 5.3.) For example, business majors may be less satisfied with electronic resources because they are unaware of all the tools that are available to them, or they could have higher demands than the rest of the user population. Such insights could indicate that additional outreach is necessary to this specific group.

Aside from discovering users' lack of awareness, LibQUAL+ can help identify problems with policies. One university I worked with found that students were very dissatisfied with group study spaces. Upon further assessment through focus groups and interviews, students mentioned that despite the availability of numerous large group rooms, the first-come policy resulted in individuals or pairs taking up the work spaces.

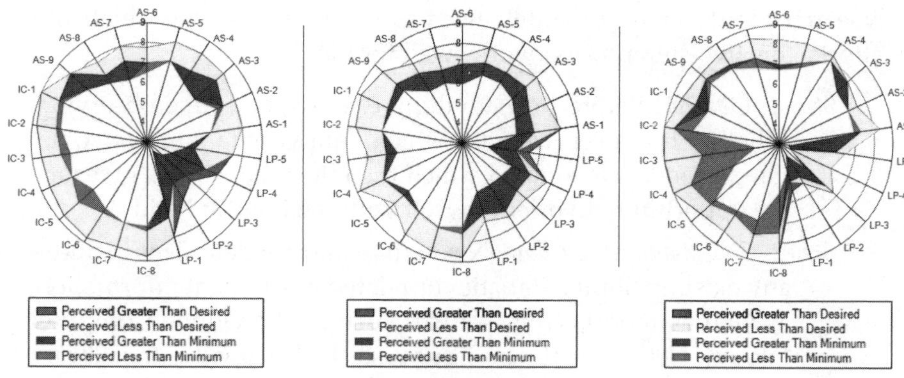

FIGURE 5.3
Georgia Tech Library LibQUAL+ results, various user groups

Since the library did not enforce any occupancy rules, students became frustrated with the process and were left feeling dissatisfied.

LibQUAL+ is a comprehensive marketing tool. When you first receive results, you may feel overwhelmed; ARL provides you with an abundance of charts, graphs, tables, numbers, and comments, but there are many excellent resources that can help you make sense out of it.[11] As an attempt to distill the results into a transparent indicator, I developed a satisfaction percentage tool, which allows you to quickly gauge your responses after entering your data into a spreadsheet.[12]

Participation in the LibQUAL+ survey costs around $2,000; however, it is definitely worth the price because of the scope of data, reliability, longitudinal value, and peer comparisons. Any academic library that is serious about marketing should include LibQUAL+ in its assessment plan.

MAKING A PLAN

Many books are dedicated to the subject of marketing research but are written for a business audience and don't easily transfer into the academic realm.[13] While there are many lessons to be learned from professional marketers, we should not feel that we have to wholeheartedly adopt or follow their strategies. Most libraries don't invest thousands of dollars or have teams of staff devoted to performing this type of research. However, we definitely need a plan in order to coordinate our efforts; this five-step process works well for me:

Step 1: Observe. Before I do anything else, I spend time observing. Whether it is a service with which I am very familiar or something brand new to me, I watch the interactions. This gives me the opportunity to orient myself with the issue at hand.

Step 2: Collect and review data. Next I dive into the data. This includes any existing library statistics or related assessment information, as well as reports from sources such as the Online Computer Library Center, ARL, or Educause. I also review the library literature and begin the process of immersion. As I explore all of this content, I keep my observations in the forefront as a basis of comparison. After noting trends, benchmarks, and major themes, I consider what else I need to know. This could include the collection of new original data through surveys or polling.

Step 3: Converse. Once I have a thorough background on the topic, I'm ready to talk with people. I include frontline staff and managers, as well as users and nonusers of the particular product, space, or service. At this point I want to test my initial observations and data, as well as continue the discovery process. I aim to receive as much information as possible, so interviews, focus groups, and follow-up inquires help fill in the details and present possibilities.

Step 4: Develop initial findings. By now I am familiar with the topic and I can begin to piece together the big picture. I look for patterns, quick fixes, missed opportunities, and areas that need serious attention. In terms of developing a communication message, I try to pinpoint the perfect audience and understand why and when they use the product. Next I distill this value into a promotional concept.

Step 5: Test the concept. Once the core elements of a promotional design are constructed (a theme, a topic, an image, a phrase, or wording), I test this concept on both the intended and unintended audience. I also gauge reactions from administrators, professors, and frontline staff. The results allow me to fine-tune the message and let me know if I completely missed the mark.

Let's look at this plan in action by continuing to apply the reference desk scenario:

Step 1. Shadow staff on the reference desk at various times of the day. Role-play the reference interview with different staff members. Study student traffic patterns near and around the desk. Observe transactions and interactions between students and librarians. Note the types of questions that are asked. Observe users throughout the entire research cycle.

Step 2. Review all available statistics and data, including telephone, e-mail, and chat reference activities. Look for patterns. Review literature and reports about reference and library trends.

Step 3. Talk with staff about the reference experience. Talk with several students after they receive reference assistance. Focus on the steps of the research process, along with student perceptions and expectations of the library and librarians. Conduct a poll around campus to gauge awareness, interest, and value of reference assistance. Talk with faculty about how they promote the library. Conduct interviews and focus group sessions with different student segments. Survey and talk with an English 101 class and one upper-level class after completing a writing assignment. Talk with librarians at peer institutions.

Step 4. Compile everything, looking for common themes. What triggers use of reference assistance? What prevents use? What are the perceptions of the library and librarians? Are there patterns or common behaviors of students conducting research? Develop a message based on these findings; this might include attributes such as awareness, timeliness, authority, convenience, ease of use, assurance, or mentoring. Select a target audience for the campaign and choose appropriate promotional channels.

Step 5. Talk with students, faculty, and library staff to test findings. Gauge reactions to marketing messages. Adjust appropriately.

The process might seem a bit elaborate, especially if there are several components that you want to research. This is why a continuous and robust thread of assessment is valuable; it enables us to evaluate numerous facets, such as quality, satisfaction, and awareness, simultaneously. What I like about this five-step process is that it builds on redundancy, making sure that you cover the story from different angles. It might not be perfect, but it gets you close enough to be effective.

In terms of promotion, however, advertising doesn't always have to be so sophisticated. Sometimes you just need to design an event flier and don't need a tremendous number of opinions on font size or clip art selection. Of course the big-picture question would be to ask, why are we hosting events? This type of study could anticipate who might attend, the ideal time and location, the best way to let people know about the event, and the types of topics or activities that are of prime interest.

The main point is that marketing research is scalable to your timeframe, budget, staff size, and abilities. While we want to be as thorough as possible, we should not invest too much time overanalyzing everything that we do. Simply asking why we do things can lead to an enlightening journey.

PUTTING THE PIECES TOGETHER

Marketing research doesn't always, if ever, divulge a clear answer. While each of these techniques adds another piece to the puzzle, what emerges is not necessarily a complete picture. This type of research points us in the direction that we need to be moving but rarely reveals a final destination. Perhaps more than anything, marketing research lets us know what we should avoid or when something definitely won't work, rather than being predictive of success.

As you sift through all of your research findings, look for the big ideas: the words, the stories, the images, and the problems that surface time and time again. These recurring themes are landmarks that should guide you; if you find a particular issue that resonates with students, let that lead you. While content that surfaces in your research is valuable, also consider the frequency, intensity, and language that bubbles forth. What is most important to your audience? This is a very subjective enterprise, so focus on the emotions, motivations, and memories that people share—make that your message.

Hopefully this summary is enough to get you started with marketing research. It's important to conduct this type of assessment before you start crafting a campaign. In chapter 10 we'll look at ways of measuring the impact of our communication activities, but for now there is one more characteristic we need to cover before we design anything: relationships. Oftentimes, the person delivering the message is equally as important as the content included. Your library needs to be entrepreneurial in building influential relationships; otherwise students may never receive your message.

NOTES

1. Edward Tufte, *The Visual Display of Quantitative Information* (Cheshire, CT: Graphics Press, 2001).
2. Stephen Porter, Michael Whitcomb, and William Weitzer, "Multiple Surveys of Students and Survey Fatigue," *New Directions for Institutional Research* 121 (2004): 63–73.
3. Ronald Powell and Lynn Connaway, *Basic Research Methods for Librarians* (Westport, CT: Libraries Unlimited, 2004).
4. Arlene Fink and Jacqueline Kosecoff, *How to Conduct Surveys: A Step-by-Step Guide* (Thousand Oaks, CA: Sage Publications, 1998); Gail Junion-Metz and Derrek Metz, *Instant Web Forms and Surveys for Academic Libraries* (New York: Neal-Schuman, 2001).
5. Howard Schultz and Dori Yang, *Pour Your Heart into It: How Starbucks Built a Company One Cup at a Time* (New York: Hyperion, 1997).
6. Richard Krueger, *Developing Questions for Focus Groups* (Thousand Oaks, CA: Sage Publications, 1998).
7. Jean Bystedt, Siri Lynn, and Deborah Potts, *Moderating to the Max: A Full-Tilt Guide to Creative, Insightful Focus Groups and Depth Interviews* (Ithaca, NY: Paramount Market Publications, 2003).
8. Georgia Tech Library, "Affinity" Focus Group Exercise, http://library commons.gatech.edu/about/docs/affinity_exercise.pdf.
9. Hy Mariampolski, *Ethnography for Marketers: A Guide to Consumer Immersion* (Thousand Oaks, CA: Sage Publications, 2006).
10. Nancy Foster and Susan Gibbons, eds., *Studying Students: The Undergraduate Research Project at the University of Rochester* (Chicago: Association of College and Research Libraries, 2008).
11. Association of Research Libraries, LibQUAL+, www.libqual.org.
12. Brian Mathews, LibQUAL+ Satisfaction Percentage Tool, http://smartech .gatech.edu/handle/1853/11424.
13. William Cohen, *The Marketing Plan* (Hoboken, NJ: Wiley, 2005); Dan Kennedy, *The Ultimate Marketing Plan* (Holbrook, MA: B. Adams, 2000); Malcolm McDonald and Adrian Payne, *Marketing Plans for Service Businesses* (Oxford: Butterworth-Heinemann, 2006); Amelia Kassel, "How to Write a Marketing Plan," *Marketing Library Services* 13 (June 1999): 5–6.

6

Building Relationships

Not many undergraduate engineering courses require literature reviews. So imagine my surprise upon discovering one; finally, a chance to show off our resources! The professor was an avid library user, but despite my best overtures he would not agree to an instruction session. He felt that research skills were something that students needed to learn earlier in the curriculum or on their own time. My big break came while helping one of his students at the information desk. After our reference encounter I created a five-minute video clip highlighting the various databases and basic strategies that we covered. The student appreciated this effort and forwarded the clip to others in his class. Over the next week I heard from several of his classmates who had follow-up questions about using particular databases and advanced search strategies. The video had piqued their interest and also caught the attention of the professor. The next semester he asked me to produce a similar clip on a different topic.

This example highlights the importance of relationships; the video was successful only because the student shared it with his peers. If I had sent the tutorial to the professor or simply placed it on the library's website, it would have been far less effective. The content alone was not enough. The context of delivery was just as important; it needed to be validated by a user. The student I helped became an advocate by lending his credibility, which garnered the interest of his classmates and his instructor. In order to get through to the faculty member, I needed a new way to package the library in a manner that didn't intrude on his lecture time. While I tried convincing him logically of the value of database instruction, the buzz of the video was what ultimately persuaded him. Many of us concentrate on outreach to faculty, hoping for a trickle-down effect, but sometimes professors need to hear about the library through their students as well.

This chapter focuses on building multilayered partnerships between a library and the community it serves. Some of these bonds are formal, while others are casual. Some develop spontaneously, and others will be sought out. The significance of these associations is twofold. First, they can help us spread information by generating positive word of mouth and expanding the reach of our communication efforts. Second, they enable us to tap into the raw and unbiased word-on-the-street evaluation of the library. This chapter demonstrates the reciprocal value that libraries gain by cultivating symbiotic partnerships with our users and others on campus.

MAKING CONNECTIONS

Great products sell themselves. Deeply satisfied customers become an unofficial sales force spreading positive reviews of items, services, or places that they find useful, entertaining, or appealing. Imagine hundreds of students talking enthusiastically about the library. While we will never be in the same echelon as the latest gadget from Apple or the trendy bar just off campus, libraries do arise in student conversations. Peer support and recommendations largely factor into decision making and can shape lasting impressions—so the reputation of your library is on the line every day. When students talk about schoolwork and assignments, library services are a part of the discussion. These unfettered strains of dialogue occur mostly outside of our control, yet it is possible to have some degree of influence. For example, knowing how information is distributed allows us to enter the conversation.

Malcolm Gladwell's famous book *The Tipping Point* provides a framework for how ideas become popular.[1] Gladwell builds on the notion that the characteristics, charisma, and credibility of the person delivering a message factors significantly into whether the content is believed, accepted, and passed on to others. He points to Paul Revere as a prime example. When the British army was approaching, Revere's famed ride alerted town leaders of the impending danger. On that same night, William Dawes also rode out, yet he failed to reach militia commanders. Gladwell emphasizes that Paul Revere was gregarious and intensely social. He was deeply involved in business, politics, and cultural circles. Since Revere was well connected throughout Massachusetts, he knew whom to tell and how to spread the news. Dawes, by contrast, did not have such an esteemed reputation or the community connections and, therefore, was unsuccessful at sounding the alarm. Here we see that the context or the delivery of messages is just as vital as the content itself.

Gladwell provides us with a system and terminology illustrating how information, trends, and behaviors are created and passed along. He examines why some things catch on and others fail. Gladwell's thesis, the law of the few, is that our society is composed of an underlying network of influential personalities that shape the beliefs of the masses. In *The Tipping Point* he spotlights three prominent character types: connectors, mavens, and salesmen. Let's look at each of them and consider how they might translate to the college campus.

Connectors are individuals like Paul Revere who have many ties in different social realms and who act as conduits of information. Think of a fraternity guy studying economics, with a minor in theater. He is connected to students in the business school, to members of Greek organizations, and to the campus artistic community. Perhaps he is also involved with a religious, charitable, academic, or civic association as well, holds an office in the student government, and works a few hours a week in the school bookstore. His social sphere spans many factions on campus. This student has abundant exposure to news and ideas, absorbing and spreading them throughout the different groups that he contacts. Connectors are like network hubs, linking people to each other and to content.

Mavens are individuals who accumulate knowledge and tend to have a strong compulsion toward helping and informing others. They are experts who stockpile information and are enthusiastic about sharing ideas. Imagine a student tuned into digital technology. He dabbles with programming, writes for several blogs, and knows about all the latest gizmos and gadgets. He uses social software extensively and relishes his reputation as geek-chic. Friends and family value his opinions and seek his tech support, and he is more than happy to share his insights. Mavens are like web servers, storing data and parsing it out.

Salesmen are persuasive individuals filled with confidence, optimism, and charisma. They influence others, often without trying. These

> are the people whom you want to work with, whom you want to be around, and whom you try to emulate. They are fascinating and leave us wanting more. Think of the homecoming queen or the student body president. Salesmen are like transmitters, social antennae pushing out content to the rest of us.

In a nutshell, the connector is the guy who knows everyone, the maven is the guy who knows everything, and the salesman is the guy whom you want to hang out with. If Paul Revere was a colonial connector, then Thomas Jefferson was a scholarly and philosophical maven, and George Washington the noble leader and salesman for the new republic.

Gladwell's archetypes are an interesting character study, but he offers little applicable direction toward developing promotional messages. It is easy to look back and dissect specific phenomena, but how can we intentionally initiate this type of system? How do we find students to fill these roles? Sometimes they will make themselves known and possibly volunteer, while other times they have to be sought out, discovered, and encouraged.

COOLHUNTING

Coolhunting applies the philosophy from *The Tipping Point* to the marketplace. Essentially, it is the practice of spotting trends early on and then integrating those concepts into commercial messages or product development. This is probably most evident in music and fashion, where the tastes of niche groups often expand to a wider audience. Coolhunters in Los Angeles, for example, noticed Latino men wearing generic bathroom slippers around the city. They alerted Converse of this emerging fashion statement, which led to the design of stylish premium slippers.[2] The objective is to anticipate or notice trends as they are forming and then cash in on them. Coolhunters attempt to predict what will become popular so that companies can embrace these emerging fads.

So how does coolhunting work? On a basic level it is glorified people watching. Coolhunters submerse themselves in the culture that they study; in the case of the youth market, this ranges from malls to MySpace. Everything that teenagers touch or interact with is noted. The advantage comes from the longevity of observation; trend spotters can see what influences particular social groups over a long period of time. This practice is derived from diffusion research, a branch of sociology that attempts to understand why certain innovations are adopted. Coolhunters strive to track down trends at the source. While they are interested in where and by whom they get started, what they really concentrate on is who is spreading the trend and who is adopting it. Gladwell's framework comes to life here: a fashion maven experiments with a new style, a connector adopts and spreads the style, which then becomes cool once a salesman starts wearing it. However, it doesn't end there. The maven must now change her style since it has become mainstream, and the cycle begins anew.

I am not suggesting that libraries should jump on every emerging trend (like Second Life, video games, or temporary tattoos) in order to entice students into using our services, but rather that a heightened awareness of campus culture will not only improve our communication efforts, but also bring us closer to the goal of becoming user-sensitive organizations. So where do we begin? Look-Look, a coolhunting firm that focuses on following youth culture, offers us a pragmatic model:[3] they rely on a network of hundreds of correspondents who log in to their website to share insights. Participants around the world contribute photos, videos, stories, slang, and other observations that they encounter in their everyday lives. These teenagers are not necessarily the trendsetters themselves, but they actively record what they see around them. This process enables Look-Look to monitor trends and influences in real time across diverse social segments and regions of the world.

The practical application of coolhunting for academic libraries is that it allows us to take the pulse of what is interesting and important to our students, provides us with opportunities for engagement, and enables us to find connectors, mavens, and salesmen within our community. Here is an example:

During the fall semester of 2007, environmental issues were front-page news; it seemed that everywhere you turned, someone was talking about green initiatives. This was especially resonant in Atlanta, where we received daily warnings about a severe drought. The need for the library to act fully materialized when I noticed three separate environmental stories in a single issue of the campus newspaper. This topic was obviously something on the minds of our students.

The traditional tactic would be to create a handout on the water crisis and include conservation tips and citations to material in the collection. I knew that this standard approach would not reach a large audience, and so instead I contacted the leaders of several student organizations. I encouraged them to think boldly, offering them thirty feet of wall space, a display case, a pin board, and a presentation stage. All of these items are located in a high-traffic zone of the library.

Together we brainstormed several ideas and I encouraged them to be surprising, even shocking, in order to grab attention. Rather than just posting doom-and-gloom statistics, they needed to create a spectacle: something that would get people talking and get their message across campus. The students were enthusiastic about this opportunity to come together from different social segments in order to collaborate on a project that interested them. Coolhunting allowed me to recognize an emerging and timely trend and to pull together a team of environmental mavens, social connectors, and campus salesmen on this venture. By building partnerships with students instead of simply treating them as transactions, academic libraries expand their role and social significance on campus.

PARTNERING WITH STUDENTS

Relationships are the key to successful communication programs. This sentiment is echoed throughout the marketing literature, where it is often stated that the emotional connection that a person feels toward products, places, or services is what truly distinguishes these items. We will explore this more concretely in chapter 7, but it's important to note that the types of relationships I'm referring to stretch beyond the typical interaction that occurs at our public service desks or in the classroom. Customer service and library instruction are important exchanges, but it is customer participation that elevates the library experience. There are many layers of partnerships that we can form with our students. Here are a few:

Advocates

Advocates are your champions, your evangelists. To some students the library is a second home, and to others it is the resources that are treasured. We may never know what draws them in—perhaps the atmosphere, the location, or simply the ideals of what a library stands for—but whatever the case may be, these advocates are valuable to us. What we need is a way to harness their sentiment and share it with others.

The most common form of formal support is student advisory groups. There are a number of variant implementations of these groups, which aim to give a voice to students pertaining to library matters.[4] These relationships offer many benefits. First and foremost they provide a forum for students to express their concerns. They may not necessarily be expert users, but members tend to be passionate about the library and can represent the student body. Another benefit to a student council is that members can serve as a sounding board for librarians and administration. This is our chance to gauge their interests, test our ideas, and gather feedback from our intended audience. We can reveal our plans to them and find out what they think. They can also help us shape promotional messages, steering us in new directions and fine-tuning the language and content that we use.

Not only do these student groups advise us, but they can help us spread information about the library. They can increase awareness about our services and lobby for our needs. There are several examples of advocacy groups raising funds for renovations, expansions, new equipment, and leisure material. By positioning the academic library as a political cause, you can unite and invigorate your students, who will become activists in your favor. We just need to give them something to believe in.

Ambassadors

The textbook strategy for generating buzz is to hire a celebrity spokesperson; your library can borrow this strategy by finding students on your campus who are quite well known. Offering them a chance to partner with the library can be mutually beneficial; it fuels their notoriety while helping us gain exposure. Many libraries use this tactic by designing *Read* posters and other print material featuring student-athletes, SGA leaders, and other achievers. However, this barely scratches the surface of what is possible.

When it comes to creating celebrities, Viacom offers a proven method: constant exposure across multiple formats reinforces audience recognition. This model is highlighted in the PBS documentary, *The Merchants of Cool,* illustrating the rise of Howard Stern.[5] While Stern refers to himself as the king of all media, it was Viacom who built the Howard Stern empire by featuring him widely across several of their media platforms. During his prime, Stern was syndicated on Viacom's Infinity radio stations, his weekly TV show was broadcast on Viacom's CBS stations, his best-selling autobiography was published by Viacom's Simon and Schuster, and his movie was released by Viacom's Paramount Pictures.

It is not surprising that Howard Stern received so much exposure, since Viacom put him in the spotlight.

MTV, another Viacom media property, employs the same celebrity-building strategy by manufacturing stars through their quasi-reality show programs. The female cast of *The Hills,* for example, has used their fame to branch off into other markets such as fashion lines, beauty products, modeling, music, event hosting, and movies. MTV no longer considers itself just a television station, but rather a content provider.[6] It aims to develop programming for all of the media formats that its audience encounters: TV, online, mobile, music, and print.

Obviously we don't have the same reach or budget as MTV, but we can use their strategy in our promotional activities. By finding students who are connectors, salesman, or mavens within various social and academic segments, we can then transform them into library ambassadors. It's not only athletes or academic achievers that we want, but a wide collection of students with diverse talents: students with a story to tell.

We'll look at selecting students a little further on, but once they are identified, place them on posters, displays, and other advertising. Interweave them throughout library campaigns. (See figure 6.1.) You can get them airtime on traditional media platforms, such as campus television or radio, and have them quoted in the school newspaper. They can also be featured in your tutorials, tours, videos, podcasts, special events, social websites, and anywhere else that the library has a presence. Similar to Viacom, our ambassadors become the public face of the library, and we can build or extend our reputation around them.

Here's an example: let's say that you find an accomplished photographer. You can feature his work in the library, possibly building a showcase event featuring several campus artists. This student can also be incorporated into your promotional material about digital cameras for checkout and the availability of photo editing software. He might also be persuaded to offer a workshop on the process of taking photos and tricks and tips for editing them afterward. The library can arrange for him to be interviewed by campus media, where he could talk about his projects and mention the related services and collections available in the library. Taking this even further, perhaps the library hosts several blogs for all its ambassadors, in which case this student could chronicle his continued photographic exploits.

Our work with these ambassadors must be more than just testimonials; it has to be about them. In the example above, the student benefits from increased exposure and solidifies himself as a photography expert,

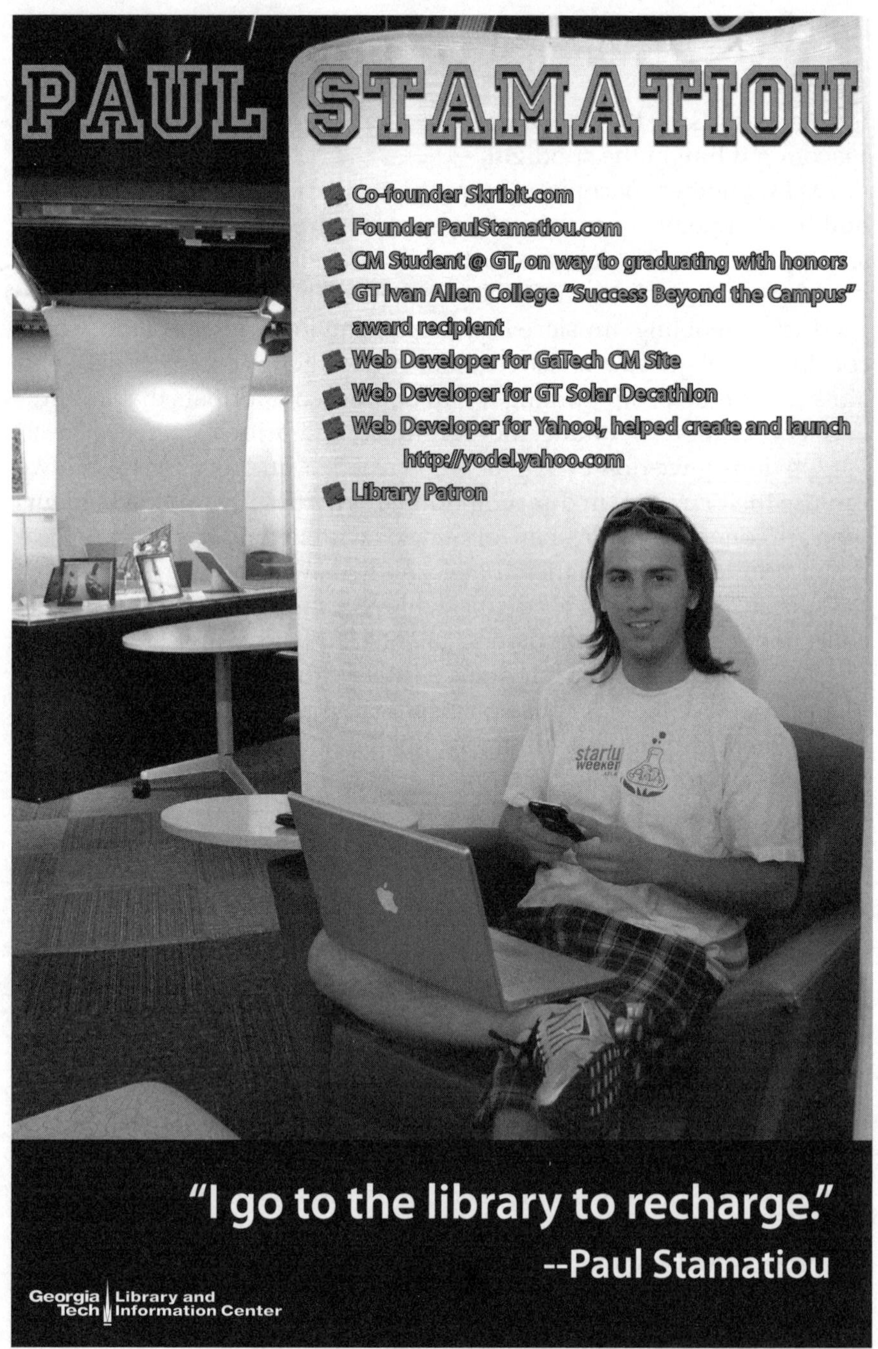

FIGURE 6.1
Student advocate poster—Paul Stamatiou

while the library gains publicity and is perceived as a cultural and creative outlet. Our strategy is to promote the talents and achievements of these students while simultaneously associating and branding them with the library.

Consultants

While advocates and ambassadors have an invested interest in the library, consultants are more like free agents or informants. They are our eyes and ears on campus. Our partnerships with them are designed to gather information, but not necessarily to push our agenda. By using students as consultants we can apply the trend-spotting model in an effort to study campus culture. Here we are not concerned about what is *cool,* but instead with the events, concerns, personalities, problems, themes, and other opportunities with which the library can become engaged. Consultants can also aid our assessment efforts, sharing explicit details about the library. These relationships enable us to find out firsthand how students use our services, along with their perceptions and awareness of our vast product inventory.

Building this network of consultants is a very imprecise system; it is more like the stitching together of personal acquaintanceships that develop over time. These are not positions that you can advertise, but rather they mature through the interactions with your community. Ideally you want to start out with several representatives from different segments. This will include a handful of students from various majors, as well as different class years. Also try to identify students belonging to diverse social circles such as international students, fraternities and sororities, artists, activists, and others mentioned in chapter 2. This ensures that you are able to cast a wide net for gathering opinions and experiences.

Diversifying has many practical applications. For example, I've spent a lot of time talking with international students, a significantly large population at Georgia Tech, in order to understand their library use. For Indian students, the library is a social hub where they can meet, interact, and mentor each other. On the other hand, Chinese and Korean students typically view the library as a place for quiet individual work. By understanding the unique expectations of different users, the library can be more conscious of their needs and communicate more personally.

Consultants can be used for gathering information on what you want to study. For example, I regularly talk with female users about their safety concerns. I rely on techies to beta test new websites and search tools, often incorporating their feedback into our design process. And we share any changes we intend to make to our physical spaces with architecture majors, seeking their input and suggestions for improvements.

While these examples illustrate how we can call on consultants for specific details, the true value in this type of program lies in the longitudinal analysis. By establishing long-term partnerships with students, we can track how their usage and perceptions change over time. Our interest here is not only in terms of the library, but also how the college experience unfolds across several years. This comprehensive insight enables us to pinpoint key moments in which students require or could take advantage of library products. Such information can greatly improve our communication strategy because we would have direct knowledge of their needs. By knowing the demands of sophomore biology majors, or the research required by a junior civil engineering major, the library can target these students. This longitudinal perception enables us to design customized messages that are aligned with the particular audience that we are trying to reach. In a nutshell, we can match the library up with key points across the curriculum and present our services incrementally as they are needed.

Affiliates

Affiliates are another important relationship for us. These are groups that work directly with students, such as teaching assistants and tutors, the writing center, the IT help desk, and academic advisors. Several campus organizations can also potentially influence campus perceptions, such as student government members, tour guides, and residential assistants. These are all vital partnerships in our communication effort.

The model we can adopt here is from publishing giant Condé Nast, which produces a vast portfolio of magazines such as *Vogue, GQ, Wired,* and the *New Yorker.* Each of these publications targets a select audience; likewise, we can tailor library news and updates accordingly.

For example, tour guides and orientation leaders might be interested in historical or quick facts about the library, as well as human interest stories, such as the person who checked out over five hundred books or the two students who *lived* in the library during finals. Student government members might be interested in policy changes or issues related to the library. We approach them in the manner of a political briefing, informing them as representatives of the student body about library business. Resident assistants, teaching assistants, and tutors will find value in the explanation of library services. Their assistance mission is similar to ours, and so we should treat them as partners in the process of aiding students.

What this really comes down to is spin. Each of these affiliate groups is likely to have an e-mail list for which you could submit content. Instead of just distributing a broad newsletter or press release, create a concise and targeted message designed for each audience. Even if the content is the same, such as the purchase of a new database, you pitch it with an appropriate context:

Tutors, teaching assistants, writing center. Be sure to tell your students about our latest database, ARTstor. This is a great tool for humanities, fine arts, and social science majors. Let us know if you'd like a demo.

Student government. The library continues to add new online resources. Based on faculty requests and student interest, we are pleased to announce the addition of ARTstor, a premier digital library of images. We are always interested in receiving student feedback and collection suggestions.

Tour guides. The library already has over two hundred online databases filled with articles, technical reports, and e-books; now we're adding art! We wanted to let you know about ARTstor, an online collection of over one million images that students can access anywhere at any time.

Another important affiliate group to consider is student media organizations: television, radio, newspaper, and possibly an activities committee. Keep in direct contact with these students and their advisors. Send members of the campus media press releases that are packaged as a scoop; these announcements should be perceived as giving insider information about changes or events as early as possible. With the ARTstor example, you might build anticipation while the contract is being signed. Send a casual e-mail informing them that the library is in the process of subscribing to a major new database, and once the ink dries provide the media outlets with the full details, emphasizing why this is newsworthy to the campus audience.

I also recommend hosting an annual lunch or dinner for student media staff, which gives them a chance to meet and interact with each other while providing the library with a forum to communicate with them directly. Be sure to have an information packet available, along with numerous ideas for potential stories.

Lastly, these students are always seeking new content, and while instinctually we want to promote the library, be sure to pass along any leads or story ideas about other units on campus as well. I find that this helps bestow a positive image of the library as a source for information.

Communicating with affiliate audiences appeals directly to their sense of obligation. Students and staff in these positions have accepted a role on campus, and it is their duty to stay informed. The library can make use of this commitment by presenting content in a manner that makes sense to them. Sending a weekly, biweekly, or monthly e-mail message, and attending live events and meetings when possible, reminds our affiliates of the library. Our goal is not to bombard them with details, but rather to pique their interest and keep the library on their minds.

FINDING PROSPECTS

There are many ways to start building your Rolodex of contacts. Although I have tried to articulate a difference among several types of formal relationships, it's not always so cut-and-dried. Often there is some overlap in participation. Someone on your advisory council might also be an ideal ambassador, or valuable consultant, by belonging to an affiliated group. What is important is to look for involvement opportunities as you interact with students. Don't worry so much about assigning them roles or titles, but instead evaluate what each person has to offer. Here are some methods that I use for finding potential communication partners:

Student Leaders

Early each fall semester I review the executive boards of all student clubs and organizations and e-mail the leaders. Depending on the size of your campus there could be hundreds of clubs, so you may want to be selective. In these e-mail messages I typically welcome them back to school and congratulate them on their posts. I also introduce myself as a representative of the library and encourage them to contact me should they have any questions. I also plant the idea that the library is open to working with student organizations—I might also provide a few examples. I make it a point to appeal to their interests instead of the library's. This initial contact often leads to further correspondence. Students seem to appreciate the attention and recognition, and club leaders can grow into helpful consultants and are usually strong connectors.

Campus Newspaper Articles

The school newspaper is more than a valuable source of campus information—it is filled with names. I make an attempt to scan every published article and note the names of featured students, faculty, and staff. This excellent source for discovering the movers and shakers on your campus is a great way to find students involved in art, politics, community projects, research, and other interesting activities. It also alerts you to the types of news, events, and issues relevant to your campus. I often send an e-mail to *newsworthy* students, opening the window for a future partnership.

Academic Department Websites

The departmental websites for schools or colleges may also highlight individual students. Often, these sites are viewed as promotional tools used to lure students into a particular field of study. A congratulatory or inquiring e-mail to these exemplary students can lead to a greater insight into how their particular discipline uses the library. Additionally, I recommend reviewing your school's admissions materials, which may spotlight extraordinary students; many of these materials even include student profiles and blogs. Contact these students, starting with a casual remark on their success, and see if they respond with any interest in the library.

The Social Web

Along with campus media and websites, the social Web invites interaction with students. Members of campus clubs and organizations can easily be found on Facebook, along with other core segments. Blogging sites like LiveJournal probably include a handful or more of your students. Tools such as Twitter can also be used to discover the personalities on your campus. These names and websites will change over time, but students make themselves fairly easy to be found online.

Feedback Forms

Many libraries include print or online feedback forms that allow students to share their comments with the library. This is a great method for identifying students who are engaged in or care about the library. Although many of them may write to complain about poor service or share their frustrations, talking with them personally about their experience can transform them into library advocates.

Assessment Projects

Assessment can be a great audition process for discovering library partners. While responses should always be kept anonymous, you can include an opportunity for students to participate in future projects. On feedback forms and surveys, or in a focus group, always include an option for participants to leave their contact information. This information creates a network of willing contributors that you can draw on for further inquiry. As you work with these students, perhaps through focus groups, polls, or interviews, you can gauge their interest level and sophistication. I view all assessment as a gateway to more meaningful relationships. Of course I don't imply that we should sign up everyone who agrees with us, but rather that this process provides us with access to insightful and compassionate students.

Permission Marketing

Seth Godin's stimulating book *Permission Marketing* challenges us to make advertising voluntary.[7] The core philosophy behind this method is that we allow potential customers to raise their hands and express interest in what we have to offer. In this sense, people become willing participants in the communication process. Students would receive invitations based on the services they use. For example, someone attending a library event could opt in to receive information about upcoming lectures or exhibits. Someone who borrows a digital camera could opt in for alerts on other library multimedia equipment and related workshops. In this manner, students subscribe to updates based on specific product lines or product portfolios. Likewise, we could parse information by discipline, dividing it by cohorts. So instead of blasting out messages to all biology majors, for example, we can target just sophomore biology students. This level of segmentation would enable us to deliver appropriate information based on the student's place within the curriculum. The objective of permission marketing is to invite students to learn more and then customize the content for them.

Recommendations

Sometimes the best way to find student volunteers is to ask those who are already helping us. Seeking referrals can be particularly useful when you are trying to target a specific segment. Students can appraise their social circles better than we can and can recommend others who might be willing to work with us.

THE PURSUIT OF PARTNERSHIPS

In this chapter my goal is to present a systematic approach toward developing partnerships with students; however, there are many others on campus whom we can work with. Clearly, faculty members also belong in this conversation. Not only are they primary users of our collections, but they are also highly influential over the students in their classes. Focus group participants regularly inform me that they learn about databases and other library resources from their professors. Faculty are a powerful word-of-mouth channel that we want to include in our marketing mix.

Many other campus units offer valuable collaborative potential, such as the health center, housing, the gym, the student center, the bookstore, the office of technology, parking and transportation, advising, counseling, performing arts, and the police, to name a few. We're only limited by our own time, imagination, and persistence.

As we strive to increase our connections on campus, it helps to embrace the social entrepreneurial spirit. Whether this involves individual students, campus clubs, support units, or professors, we should always be on the lookout for strategic alliances. In my experience, people tend to be open to working with libraries because of our dedication to the academic agenda; but while obviously we have our own interests in mind, it is tactful to consider how others might benefit from us. For example, the writing center might be able to reach more students if they had an office in the library. Most of us make it our core mission to assist users in finding information; however, we can extend this by aiding the pursuits of others on campus. Whether this is the housing office, the chemistry department, or the glee club, we should keep asking ourselves how we can help make others successful.

Libraries are perfectly positioned to be brokers on campus; we connect people not only with resources and scholarly materials, but also to each other. Libraries bring people together for academic, cultural, creative, and social causes; no one else on campus so completely fulfills that role. And so it is vital that we try to be visible on campus, not just as salesman pitching our products, but as participants. Library representatives have much to gain by attending campus events, meetings, lectures, and activities. I have found the dining hall, sporting events, and art exhibits to be invaluable places for building and nurturing campus partnerships. I even golfed once with a department chair and played video games against resident assistants in order to garner goodwill for the library. These informal conversations take us outside of our librarian-provider role and allow us to be more approachable. Let's be honest: most people don't understand what exactly a librarian does, so these encounters help lay the foundation of understanding. Similarly, interacting with students, faculty, and staff through blogs, Facebook, Twitter, and other social web tools fosters a friendly and personal connection. As we aspire to be user-sensitive organizations, we should not see library users as mere customers, patrons, transactions, statistics, or web hits, but instead view them as students with unique needs, problems, talents, opinions, preferences, and suggestions.

NOTES

1. Malcolm Gladwell, *The Tipping Point: How Little Things Can Make a Big Difference* (Boston: Back Bay Books, 2002).
2. Peter Gloor and Scott Cooper, *Coolhunting: Chasing Down the Next Big Thing* (New York: AMACOM, 2007).
3. FRONTLINE, *The Merchants of Cool,* "Interview: Dee Dee Gordon and Sharon Lee," www.pbs.org/wgbh/pages/frontline/shows/cool/interviews/gordonandlee.html.
4. Amy Deuink and Marianne Seller, "Students as Library Advocates," *College and Research Libraries News* 67 (Jan 2006): 18–21; Michael Smith and Leslie Reynolds, "The Street Team: An Unconventional Peer Program for Undergraduates," *Library Management* 29 (2008): 145–58; Candace Benefiel, Wendi Arant, and Elaine Gass, "A New Dialogue: A Student Advisory Committee in an Academic Library," *Journal of Academic Librarianship* 25 (Mar 1999): 111–13; ASU Libraries, Arizona State University, "Library Student Advisory Committee," Arizona Board of Regents, http://lib.asu.edu/

stuadvis/; Gelman Library, George Washington University, "Gelman Library Student Liaison," www.gwu.edu/gelman/library/liaison/.

5. Barak Goodman and Rachel Detzin, *The Merchants of Cool* (Boston: PBS Home Video, 2003).
6. Brian Mathews, "On Being Platform Agnostic: Jason Hirschhorn Presentation," *ALT-REF* blog, http://altref.blogspot.com/2006/03/on-being-platform-agnostic.html.
7. Seth Godin, *Permission Marketing: Turning Strangers into Friends, and Friends into Customers* (New York: Simon and Schuster, 1999).

7 Developing Brand Strategies

I love the game of golf even though I am a terrible player. Despite taking lessons, reading instructional books, and spending hours at the driving range, I've never developed a decent swing. A few years ago I purchased a Nike driver, the same club that Tiger Woods uses, and although I wish I could say that my skills increased dramatically, this wasn't the case. While my game might not have improved, my perspective has; now, every time I step up to the tee I *believe* that I can hit it a mile. That is the power of branding. Using Nike equipment fills me with confidence and makes me feel like an official PGA player, even if my ball ends up in the water hazard.

Branding is perhaps the most enigmatic component of marketing. A tremendous amount of material has been published on the topic, with everyone adding their own twist on the idea. If your library intends to develop a large-scale and expensive brand campaign, then I highly recommend reading books written by experts in the field.[1] My intention is simply to provide you with a basic branding foundation and to guide you through several practical examples that you can incorporate into your communication efforts.

What branding really boils down to is the distinction between items. How is product A different from product B? Brand is what separates *luxury* from *middle of the line* from *generic.* The brand messaging is a strategy that asserts a unique characteristic of a product. This claim—or promise as it is typically referred to—is based on a distinguishing attribute such as price, prestige, authenticity, exclusivity, convenience, ease of use, speed, special features, reliability, or quality. In this chapter we will look at how we can use marketing strategies to emphasize the value of library products and align them with user needs.

DEFINING BRAND

First things first: you can't control your brand. You can shape it, push it, adjust it, or influence it, but you don't own it. Your brand lives in the minds of the users; it is your reputation. While we can make claims and offer evidence of what we stand for, it is ultimately up to users to decide the significance of the library. Another way of thinking about brand is to consider all the mental associations that get stirred up when you hear or think about a particular product or company.[2] Take Disney for example: whether it is the movies, the television channel, or the amusement parks, their overarching theme is family-oriented entertainment. This is their brand concept; it's who they are and what they stand for, and their products live up to the hype.

As we plan to apply this strategy to our libraries, it is important to note the difference between the brand (the philosophical concept of who we are and what we offer) and the branding (the visual representation of our services). Brand represents the idea, while branding is the recognizable image. Another way to put it, the brand is a descriptive noun (the premier sports equipment and apparel company in the world), and branding is a graphical and textual translation of this concept (Tiger Woods, the Nike swoosh, and "Just do it!"). Branding is what makes the product identifiable: the name, symbol, tagline, or design.

In their definitive marketing textbook, Kotler and Armstrong illustrate brand strategy as follows: a customer might assume that an expensive bottle of perfume is of high quality, yet if the same scent were sold in an unmarked bottle, it would likely be viewed as a lesser product.[3] This perception is what the brand provides; it makes us think that something is top of the line (brand) because of its high price and designer name (branding).

Taking this example even further, I could create a scent called Bibliotheca and in my promotion call it "the signature scent for librarians." By making this statement, I instantly plant the first flag in a new niche market. Someone else could then come along and sell Numérique, the "preferred scent of next-gen or 2.0 librarians." Here they would enter into my product category (perfume for librarians) and divide it up by reaching a particular segment of my target population. My competitors could also make the claim that my perfume is old-fashioned or outdated, while theirs is hip and more youthful as an attempt to distance their product from mine.

Obviously this example is a bit silly and oversimplifies the process, but hopefully it illustrates the practice of brand strategy. You stake your claim and deliver on it, and then users will either adopt or reject the idea. Consider the Nike swoosh, the Starbucks siren, and McDonald's arches. These symbols (the branding) are instantly recognized by consumers. The brand concept describes their overall identity: a premium sports apparel and equipment company, the premier neighborhood coffeehouse, and a family-oriented fast-food restaurant. So in this discussion about brands, we have to consider both the reputation (the concept) as well as the representation (the visual image) of the product or service. A brand strategy helps consumers identify who we are and what we do.

The core objective when developing a brand strategy is that it needs to be relatable to the intended audience. It should separate or differentiate the product in the user's mind. If we are doing our job correctly, the brand message will not only tell users about the library, but also make them want to use it. While it is easy to get caught up in the high-minded rhetoric of libraries, such as the "gateway to information," in order to be effective we may need to simplify our message. Treat the development of brand concepts as having a casual discussion with a student or whomever you want to reach. What do you emphasize? What tone do you take? And how do you persuade them?

THE THREE LAYERS OF BRAND STRATEGY

We'll be able to use this technique as a better way to frame and describe our services, resources, and spaces. We want to make our products stand out and align them with particular courses and student needs. I have found the best way to approach this marketing strategy is to look at branding as three separate layers: the visual layer, the value layer, and the emotional layer. By interweaving these three levels we can craft a more complete brand picture.

Visual. The visual element on which most people focus is the logo that we place everywhere, or the slogan that we write, such as "connecting you to the world of information" or "the place that makes you think!" Think of the Nike swoosh and "Just do it!"

This visual layer consists of the graphics and text that we use to *represent* ourselves and our services publicly.

Value. This is our appeal to our users. It is the blending of facts and perceptions that we want to portray. The value layer attempts to reach users on an intellectual level, making a case for why they should use the library. Examples might include: over one hundred computers and thirty software programs so you can work on assignments, group study rooms so you can practice presentations, or a silent reading room for when you need to review notes. These statements place a value on the functionality of our products. They are not intended to be advertising slogans, but to illustrate a rational quality that we can build into our messaging. Simply put, this is how we want students to *think* about the library.

Emotional. The third layer of branding is the emotional connection. This is where we implant the impression of desirability. Nike marketing presents equipment as premier sports products; however, Calloway, Titlist, and PING are also top-of-the-line golf brands. In this instance, quality is equal, but what makes Nike more appealing to me is their youthful spirit. While the other brands are obviously also professional grade, I associate them with my grandfather's era. What sets Nike apart is that they make golf cool. In this sense, the brand idea is transcendent; more than just the logo and a claim of quality, it is something that becomes aligned with our own identity. What we want to do is trigger this type of psychological sensation. *Why study alone at home when the library is filled with people who can help you?* Or, *Google is great for finding information, but the library is designed for research.* With this layer we can address how we want students to *feel* about the library.

Assembling these three layers gives us a well-rounded approach to forming a brand strategy. By combining all the pieces we are able to present a visual, valuable, and emotional message to our audience. This framework can be applied to the core mission of the library, an overarching message, as well as to particular products or product lines. Think about how you might describe library space, library assistance services, library supplies and equipment, or the library collection. By developing a brand identity for different bundles of items in our inventory, we can craft messages that appeal to particular user segments.

For example, if we target students with group projects, we can show people using different library services along with a slogan "The library is where groups come together." This works in a literal sense, in which the library is a physical building where students gather, but also in a more philosophical manner in which individuals become a team by working on their assignment together. We emphasize the value of the library as a place designed for group work: meetings, brainstorming, writing, research, assembling, and rehearsing. And our emotional appeal is that the library is the ideal location on campus for academic collaborations; it has "everything you need" and it is "the place for groups."

Let's use the reference desk as another example. We portray a student approaching the counter pulling a wagon filled with notes, textbooks, and papers. The slogan reads, "Ask us anything." The value we want to depict is that the library has experts in every discipline. With every class and every assignment, we can help you get started. The emotional appeal is reassurance and encouragement. In the background of the image, other students lug their books in wheelbarrows or carry huge piles of materials. Our core concept is that "you are not alone"; college is a lot of work, literally represented by the load they carry, but others are in the same boat. Librarians are not only available to help, but there is precedence; we have helped hundreds of students working on that very same assignment. Our message is that librarians are not only knowledge experts, but experienced people that students can trust and rely on to help guide them along the way.

BRANDING PRODUCTS

Brand strategy helps us to create a meaningful identity for library items that will make sense to our users. For example, if your library includes large-format printing, this service might be of little interest to the majority of undergraduates. However, for architecture majors who need to produce blueprints or engineering students who need to present poster sessions, this is a desirable service. Much of what branding is really about is establishing a distinction between items. It is a commercial battlefield wherein rivals try to one-up each other: Coke vs. Pepsi, Apple vs. Microsoft, McDonald's vs. Burger King. In our case, however, branding is a great tool for introducing our product portfolio and helping students to recognize the advantage in what we have to offer.

Branding is our opportunity to embrace one of the classic adages of marketing: find a niche and fill it. We want the library to be the first thing that comes to mind when students encounter particular academic needs. Our objective is to frame or position our products in such a way that they become the obvious choice to users. *I need to design and print a poster for class, so of course I go to the media studio in the library.*

Let's look at how we can use this technique. Take a look at your product inventory from chapter 4 and apply the three layers of branding to each item. Don't feel that you need to develop a full-blown campaign—this is just a conceptual exercise—but consider a concise brand identity for particular resources, services, spaces, and product categories. Our objective is to uncover which student segments would be most interested in and likely to use the different products that we offer. Don't forget to consider motivation as well as value. Here are a few examples to get you started:

Databases

Visual "Why search anywhere else?" A large pile of print journals are connected via wires to a computer. The screen displays a simple search interface and links to PDF documents.

Value Millions of articles at your fingertips.

Emotional Research is easy when you look in the right place.

Quiet study space

Visual "The best view on campus." An attempt at irony here, the image is a quintessential library desk filled with books, notes, and a laptop. It is secluded, yet warm and comfortable. To the side is a large window with a spectacular view of the campus.

Value Everything you need to study.

Emotional The library has a chair for you. No distractions—just you and everything you need.

Reference librarians

Visual "Even your professor needs help from time to time." Show images of faculty from different disciplines working with librarians on their work.

Value Librarians are experts at research.

Emotional Librarians are your inside source; they've helped hundreds with assignments over the years.

Leisure materials

Visual "You never know what you'll find." William Shakespeare, Wolfgang Amadeus Mozart, Dave Chappelle, and Spider-Man are seated in your library's café. Feel free to substitute other cultural icons.

Value While the library is primarily a scholarly resource, many DVDs, CDs, video games, comics, and fiction books are available for checkout.

Emotional The library collection offers something for everyone.

Help

Visual "Find help in the library." A student stands at the help desk. Behind the counter are several individuals wearing different labels: a librarian, a teaching assistant, an IT guy, a peer, a writing center instructor, an advisor, a math tutor, and a coffee barista.

Value The library offers a suite of assistance services; it is a full-service center.

Emotional Whatever you need, there is someone here who can help you.

While you can design these types of messages for each item in your portfolio, we can also try to fill niche areas on campus. Through careful observation you might discover opportunities in which the library can play a new role on campus. In marketing, this potential is referred to as the *white space,* an area that is currently unfilled. One example might be to position the library as the central place for student and faculty engagement on campus, in which events and programming are instituted for casual and interdisciplinary discourse between professors and undergrads outside of the classroom. Another possibility is to present the library as the place for group work on campus and back up that claim by highlighting the appropriate spaces and services.

White space can also be less abstract. A university I worked with had no central IT office on campus and, consequently, no instructional design support. This was an excellent opportunity for the library to expand its role by offering faculty assistance with Blackboard, developing course tools, tutorials, and other learning objects. Look around for these white-space opportunities; when you discover a void, consider how the library might fill it.

THE BIG VISION

Crafting messages for specific products enables us to be more descriptive and to target different segments. However, we can also use branding to develop an overarching theme that encapsulates everything we do. This is the big vision that unifies all of your communication messages. While this approach definitely takes more time and effort, the payoff is a centralized, brand-driven campaign.

Let's look at some possible big-picture concepts that you could apply to your library. These examples have developed through numerous student focus groups and interviews, and while they are probably universal, I strongly encourage you to conduct your own marketing research in order to find unique themes for your community.

Productivity

Based on the research methods of Clotaire Rapaille, I have gathered more than two hundred responses from college students around the United States, after asking them to share their strongest memory or impression of their library.[4] The common theme that emerged from these stories was a sense of accomplishment. While a few students noted frustrations or confusion with the library, the vast majority of respondents mentioned the library in their preparations for academic achievement: the ritual of reviewing notes in the reading room just before a test, pulling an all-nighter to finish a paper, writing and rehearsing a group presentation the week that it was due, or studying together with friends. The library is the place on campus where schoolwork gets done. Such a revelation may sound a bit obvious to us, but this theme of productivity is on target with users. Your brand concept could be to demonstrate the variety and diversity of scholarly tasks and assignments that can be completed in the library.

The Third Place

The philosophy of the "third place" outlined in Oldenburg's *The Great Good Place* highlights the need for and the value of public destinations that are between work and home.[5] Starbucks has famously embraced this concept in their branding efforts to be not only the premier coffeehouse, but an inviting neighborhood gathering spot as well. For the campus community, the library could potentially serve this function.

While there are other meeting places on campus, such as dorms, parks, student centers, restaurants, and bookstores, it is the academic library that offers the core qualities of the third place philosophy. Libraries are typically neutral and central locations open to all students. The inclusion of cafés has reshaped perceptions, making our buildings appear less restrictive. Libraries have also evolved into mixed-use spaces that can accommodate a variety of activities: socializing, lectures and presentations, art and displays, studying, brainstorming, and relaxing. Libraries are places for casual conversations, events and programs, collaborative work, and of course an assortment of academic endeavors. The brand concept for this theme becomes the multifaceted layers of the academic library.

Peers

Another dominant theme that surfaced in my marketing research was the importance of peers. One of the biggest draws of the library was the guarantee that other students would be there. On many campuses, the library is a place to see and be seen. Beyond this social benefit, students also described the library as an academic commune. I found a continuous thread in the idea of feeling inspired by the presence of others engaged in a similar pursuit. *We are all in this together.* In this vein, libraries provide a sense of positive peer pressure in which students subconsciously encourage and motivate each other. Many students also described working together with friends; even though they might be studying different disciplines, a definite bonding experience occurs in libraries. Peer mentoring is another tangent of this concept. Students mentioned that they could often find someone in their major when they needed help or clarification on an assignment or reading. The library provides a space where students can interact. The brand concept for this theme is about bringing people together; you never know whom you'll run into in the library.

Refuge

While to some the library is a place for collaboration, to others it is a place for escape. This idea is frequently described with imagery of the solemn stacks and the silence they offer. However, when you get to the essence of this idea, the library is a place to focus. It is a place to recharge, to realign, and to reset priorities. Libraries afford a sense of anonymity, allowing students to disappear for a few hours, to get away from the noise and distractions of life. The brand concept for this theme might channel the meditative qualities of the library and the Zen of scholarly realization.

Therapy

The academic library might even possess some therapeutic qualities. Think of it as the place to go for academic problems. When students get bogged down or the semester gets too stressful, an evening in the library can help overcome this strain. Some students even described trips to the library as a religious or spiritual experience in which they are seeking penance for slacking off, and that through hours of devotion to studying or research, they can make amends and get back on track.

There is also a psychological transformation that occurs when someone enters a library; they are transported into a different mindset. Some students describe this as a sanctuary dedicated to scholarship, a place that puts them in the mood for doing research, reflecting, and writing. Being surrounded by books and other students working dutifully creates an inspiring environment. The brand concept here should tap into the idea of rejuvenation and empowerment.

Self-Discovery

The theme of discovery is another possible concept, playing into the traditional role of libraries being temples of knowledge. In a modern sense, the library also functions like a laboratory—a place where the information that is covered in the classroom, read in textbooks, and found through research begins to make sense. Intellectually speaking, it is while in the library that students find meaning in the materials. Libraries are a test bed for new ideas, intellectual curiosity, and experimentation and where the prep work for class is conducted. And it is in the library where academic progress unfolds: writing papers, preparing presentations, designing websites, reading texts, brainstorming in group meetings, and working on assignments. In this manner, the library becomes the ultimate place for self-improvement, self-discovery, and self-assurance. Every time you visit the library you leave knowing more. The brand concept here is presenting the library as a place where knowledge is not only collected, but also applied, and where students achieve a sense of fulfillment as their work is completed.

As I mentioned earlier, branding at this level is a huge enterprise. It should not develop solely through staff meetings, but parsed out through conversations and interactions with your users. Talk with students and listen to the language, imagery, and experiences that they reveal about your library. This is the seed from which your brand should blossom.

THE BRAND AND LIBRARY STAFF

Branding can be an internal tool as well. This approach can be used to align staff with a strategic vision. Coca-Cola uses "make every drop matter" for its corporate campaign. This slogan builds on the idea of employee commitment to every customer, but can also be read as the unity of the organization: everyone plays a part and everyone matters.

There is a big difference in the way that an organization views itself, compared to the image it projects outwardly. You don't want to confuse these roles in your communication efforts. Library administration might refer to the library as the "gateway of knowledge" or "the heart and soul of the campus" as a means of coordinating the overall vision; however, these themes might not particularly appeal to undergraduate students. When developing a brand identity, be sure that you know your audience.

MCDONALD'S AND THE LIBRARY BRAND

I think that McDonald's provides an ideal model for libraries to follow. While some criticism and concern have been raised about nutrition and operational practices, their branding strategy is a remarkable success. John Love's *McDonald's: Behind the Arches* chronicles the evolution of the restaurant's empire.[6] In the early years McDonald's focused on speedy service as their distinguishing attribute. Next they boasted about quantity, listing how many millions of burgers had sold. However, with so many other fast-food restaurants in the marketplace, McDonald's needed to separate itself and ran regional promotions that emphasized taste, consistency, affordability, location, and cleanliness. These tactics worked for a while, but other franchises kept pace. It was in the 1970s that McDonald's launched a nationwide television campaign, unheard of at that time for a restaurant, and focused on the enjoyment of the McDonald's experience, rather than the food itself. McDonald's claimed to be about bringing together family and friends and transformed itself into the $22 billion a year corporation that it is today.

McDonald's foresight is admirable because it focused on the idea of making the dining experience fun. Families, looking for more than just an affordable meal, want to spend time together, and McDonald's, like Disney theme parks, has something for everyone. This inclusive vision holds strong today. McDonald's maintains its core menu of burgers and fries but has also introduced salads and healthy dishes, along with gourmet coffee and baked goods. There is the drive-through for on-the-go service and a clean, comfortable, and colorful interior for extended dining. They offer play areas, Happy Meals, and kid-friendly seating, as well as lounge chairs, televisions, newspapers, and Wi-Fi access.

McDonald's provides us with a valuable lesson about branding: the power of emotion. While there are many interesting aspects about the restaurant chain, it is the versatility that makes it so appealing. Similarly, academic libraries strive to be many things to many people. We highlight our quality collections, our quick and easy online access tools, our diverse study and work spaces, and our helpful assistance, but is this effort enough? Although we present our products and services logically, emphasizing their benefits, we may be missing out on the big picture. The library is connected to everything that students encounter in the classroom. While McDonald's brings people together for food and fun, we bring them together for academic success. By showing how our products are aligned with specific courses, assignments, and student needs, the library can transcend being just a study hall and book warehouse and transform itself into an engaging part of the college experience. We are partners in student productivity, a scholarly workshop, and an intellectual amusement park. That is the power of branding.

Our next step is to look at how we can deliver our message. We can use many promotional building blocks to communicate with students. Developing a brand concept is one piece of the puzzle, but reaching our intended audience is another critical part of the marketing process.

NOTES

1. Alina Wheeler, *Designing Brand Identity: A Complete Guide to Creating, Building, and Maintaining Strong Brands* (Hoboken, NJ: Wiley, 2003); Alice Tybout and Tim Calkins, eds., *Kellogg on Branding: The Marketing Faculty of the Kellogg School of Management* (Hoboken, NJ: Wiley, 2005); Martin Lindstrom, *Brand Sense: Build Powerful Brands through Touch, Taste, Smell, Sight, and Sound* (New York: Free Press, 2005); Geoffrey Randall, *Branding: A Practical Guide to*

Planning Your Strategy (London: Kogan Page, 2000); Al Ries and Laura Ries, *Twenty-two Immutable Laws of Branding: How to Build a Product or Service into a World-Class Brand* (New York: Harper Business, 2002); Daryl Travis, *Emotional Branding: How Successful Brands Gain the Irrational Edge* (Roseville, CA: Prima Venture, 2000); Elisabeth Doucett, *Creating Your Library Brand: Communicating Your Relevance and Value to Your Patrons* (Chicago: American Library Association, 2008).

2. Lindstrom, *Brand Sense.*
3. Philip Kotler, *Principles of Marketing* (Upper Saddle River, NJ: Prentice Hall, 2001).
4. Clotaire Rapaille, *Culture Code: An Ingenious Way to Understand Why People around the World Live and Buy as They Do* (New York: Broadway, 2006).
5. Ray Oldenburg, *The Great Good Place: Cafés, Coffee Shops, Community Centers, Beauty Parlors, General Stores, Bars, Hangouts, and How They Get You through the Day* (New York: Marlowe, 1997).
6. John Love, *McDonald's: Behind the Arches* (New York: Bantam Books, 1995).

8

Promotional Building Blocks

A common marketing maxim is that it often takes five impressions before an advertisement is effective, implying that you would have to drive by a billboard several times before you absorb the content. The flip side of this principle, though, is the saturation point. After extended exposure, consumers begin to ignore the message; the billboard fades into the background of their daily commute. This struggle for the consumer's attention is the foundation of advertising. It is a delicate balance between keeping materials fresh and visible long enough to have an impact, yet not so long that they become stagnant and unseen.

We need to be especially creative and tactical with our promotional efforts because the concept of *the library* is already present in students' minds. Our challenge is to build on initial expectations while expanding their perception of what an academic library has to offer. One advantage that we have over a corporation or a marketing firm is close proximity to a well-defined population. It is much easier for us to observe, interact, and react to our users; however, we can't take their familiarity for granted. Simply hanging a poster in a busy area is not an effective enough strategy. Instead, we need to find multiple ways to make an impression.

BUILDING BLOCKS

Think about how your local car dealership typically advertises. It buys television, radio, and newspaper ads; sends out direct mail; and occasionally hosts sales events. Each individual component contributes to the total advertising effort. This marketing mix, as it is commonly known, represents the full collection of promotional pieces that make up a campaign. All of these different elements function like building blocks, working together to deliver an integrated and widely distributed message.

For a library-specific example, let's say that your institution provides a site license for EndNote bibliographic software. Your promotional efforts might include information on your library's website, a poster near a computer cluster, and a mention of the citation software during library instruction sessions. The use of the website, print, and the classroom interaction compose your marketing mix.

A student might first encounter the EndNote poster, but since he doesn't understand what it is, he ignores it. A few weeks later a librarian mentions EndNote during a class. The next time that the student walks by the poster, he recognizes the name of the software, but still doesn't associate it with a direct need. As the semester progresses, the student visits the library's website, seeking information on how to cite his articles. He comes across the EndNote page, but discovers that he needs to install the software and opts out. The next day he talks with a classmate who mentions that EndNote is available on the library computers. Later that evening, he gets help from a librarian and formats his paper appropriately.

This example illustrates the importance of continued exposure using a variety of formats. By utilizing numerous promotional materials and spreading them over the course of time, visibility is greatly increased. Remember, our goal is for five impressions. Each promotional initiative that you build should consider vertical and horizontal progression. (See figure 8.1.) The vertical line is the stack of promotional channels that you intend to use (posters, website, instruction sessions), whereas the horizontal line represents the sequence of time over which the materials are presented to the audience (week 2, week 5, week 12).

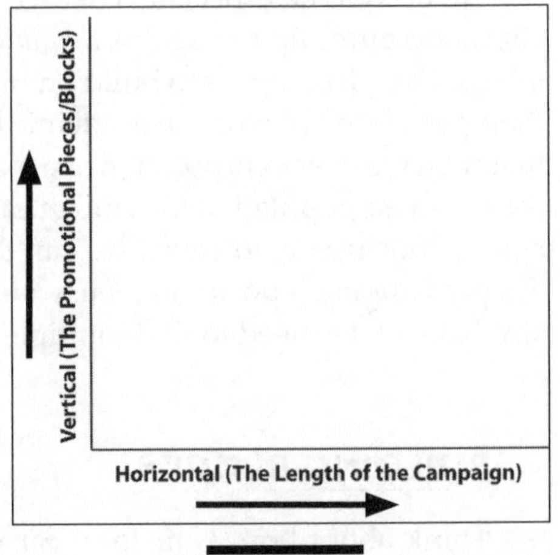

FIGURE 8.1
Marketing campaign axis

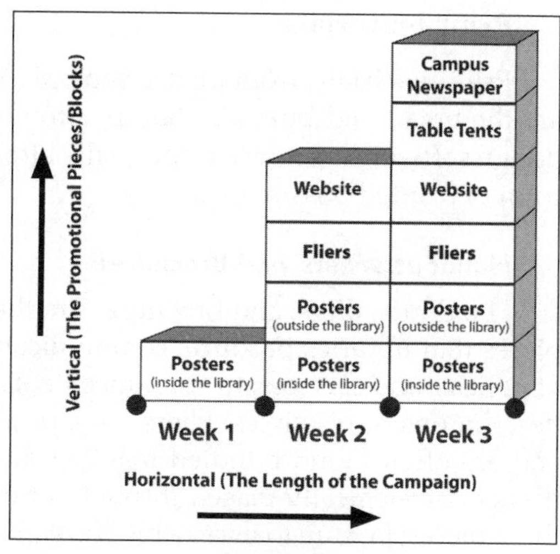

FIGURE 8.2
Promotional building blocks

Combining these factors allows us to plot our communication strategy.

Let's say that you have a library event that you intend to promote; it could be a guest speaker, a workshop, a gaming night, or a film viewing. Figure 8.2 illustrates a basic approach that you might use to get the word out. You will want to initiate the campaign three weeks before the date in order to build interest. In week one you start by hanging a poster at the front of the library announcing the event. During week two you add additional print materials in appropriate locations around campus, place fliers at the public service desk, and add the event to your library's website. The third week builds on the foundation by adding table tents in the café and a blurb in the school newspaper.

Proper planning allows for mounting exposure and anticipation as the event draws near. By using numerous types of promotional materials, visibility increases for your regular library users, as well as potentially piquing the interest of less frequent visitors. This horizontal and vertical scheme facilitates effective campaign management, enabling you to sequence the series of impressions that you distribute to your audience.

SELECTING THE MIX

Selecting the right marketing mix is an important step in message design. There is a wide assortment of promotional pieces that you can employ. This overview highlights the most common communication strategies used by academic libraries.[1] These are the channels that we will use to reach our customers.

Print Materials

Print materials, from glossy showpieces to photocopied handouts, are the bread and butter of library promotions. Desktop printing and design software are now exceptionally affordable, enabling a wide spectrum of printed possibilities.

Handouts, Fliers, and Brochures

Handouts, fliers, and brochures are the most common promotional pieces that libraries produce, communicating topics from explanations of policies and services, to announcements of events and workshops, to descriptions of resources. Fliers are a primary communication channel and are often found bundled together at service points and entranceways or strategically placed throughout the building. When designing these pieces, be sure to inject a bit of creativity. An effective approach we used at Georgia Tech was to describe the supplies and equipment that the library offers in the form of a take-out menu.[2]

Visual elements should factor strongly into your design, because too much text can be a deterrent. Segmentation might also play into your concept; consider the difference in presenting the library to incoming freshmen verses incoming graduate students. Because fliers are easy to produce, there is a danger of saturation; you probably don't want to turn your library into a cluttered Times Square.

Bookmarks

Bookmarks are another library staple. Because libraries are in the book business, users practically expect us to offer bookmarks. These items are often printed on heavy stock paper, sometimes full-color and glossy, and are stacked at the circulation desk, conveniently available when users check out a book. Typical information adorning bookmarks includes the library's website URL, phone number, e-mail address and instant messenger name, floor plans, collection information, call numbers, service point locations, and fun facts. Although library bookmarks may be a bit clichéd, adding memorable content featuring student-athletes, comic strips, or unusual or thematic photography can greatly enhance their appeal and collectibility.

Posters and Banners

Access to a large-format printer can greatly enhance your library's promotional capabilities. These high-end machines range from $2,000 to $6,000 and can produce full-color, movie-poster-size prints or fabric banners. These posters are versatile and can be used for highlighting services, announcing new resources, and promoting events. Compared with handouts or fliers, posters have a much more dramatic effect, creating a greater sense of spectacle and legitimacy; a high-quality poster will guarantee at least a casual glance. If you intend to distribute posters or fliers around campus, be sure to check with facilities managers first to prevent materials from being taken down.

Table Tents

I like to think of table tents as an exclamation point for a campaign; they can supplement other forms of communication and add a real punch. These mini-displays rest on tables, desks, or counters, presenting double-sided information so that people sitting across from each other can all view it. Table tents can appear tacky, especially if they are laden with clip art or if they overstay their welcome. I suggest using table tents for no more than two weeks and strategically placing them around the library, thereby preventing a cluttered appearance.

Maps and Floor Plans

Libraries are not always the easiest buildings to navigate. Handouts of floor plans are often created to help students find their way around the stacks. These maps can also highlight service points, study areas, computer clusters, and other features of interest. Since these guides are typically used by students in the pursuit of books or journals, you might also consider including information about core databases, research assistance, and any equipment that is available to users.

Newsletters

Newsletters provide an effective way to keep users informed about updates and changes to the library. Although these types of bulletins have largely become digital communications, printed copies are still effective. Placing these periodic updates at the circulation desk, near the front door, or even in the bathroom stalls can result in surprisingly wide readership. Copies might also be delivered to on-campus students directly through their dorms. Separate newsletters are also commonly produced for faculty and alumni audiences.

Napkins

Napkins present an intriguing opportunity for advertising and, similar to table tents, are great supplemental outlets. They could be distributed in your library's café or "donated" to your campus dining hall. Customized napkins are very affordable, with prices around $300 for ten thousand one-color designs. These could be used to promote reference services by highlighting intriguingly unusual questions, upcoming events or workshops, or simply fun facts about the library. Don't try to cover anything too serious.

Giveaways

Everyone loves getting something for free, whether it's a food sample at a grocery store or pens at a conference. Libraries offer an abundance of freebies including T-shirts, pens, calendars, key chains, magnets, stress balls, USB drives, water bottles, coffee mugs, rulers, compasses, and Frisbees. These items typically include a library logo along with the website URL and contact information. The objective of these promotional pieces is to remind students of the library and to encourage them to make it a part of their regular routine.

Coupons are another way to drum up business. If your library has a café or vending service, consider providing discounts throughout the semester. You can develop themes, such as discounts for freshmen the first week of the fall semester or free bagels for physics majors on Einstein's birthday. Discounts don't necessarily have to be food-related, but might also include free printing or photocopying, overdue book forgiveness, or other incentives during specific days and times. Giveaways, discounts, and other offerings are a great way to generate positive exposure and to get people talking about the library.

Events

More goes on in academic libraries than just research, studying, and web surfing. Students have a broad spectrum of needs, and the library can fill a large role in the student experience. We want to find ways of bringing them in, keeping them there, and making them want to return.

Orientations and Welcome Events

Most colleges offer an orientation for new students. These sessions are jam-packed with information, and library content likely becomes a blur. For many students, though, these sessions may be the first time they hear about the library. What they are told establishes their first impression. If you are unable to obtain face time with these incoming students, then be sure to provide your academic departments with key selling points and information packets to hand out.

Additionally, many academic libraries host their own orientation sessions during the initial weeks of the semester. Free food and drinks are a common lure to get students in to hear about services and resources and to tour facilities. Open house events are another way to attract students. The mixture of food, games, and social encounters is a great opportunity to increase student exposure to the library.

Instruction and Workshops

Instructional sessions are a central part of an academic library's mission. Teaching students how to navigate the databases, to locate books, and to select and cite appropriate information is a core component. While many of these sessions are embedded in the classroom, supplemental workshops and subject-based instruction classes are often held in the library throughout the semester. Aside from research orientations, classes on using software, multimedia programs, and specialized resources and equipment will often spark interest.

Games

Many libraries provide an assortment of leisure materials in the form of books, DVDs, and music, so video games represent a natural evolution. Not only are academic libraries including video games in their collections, but they are also letting students play in the building and are organizing tournaments. However, games don't always have to be electronic; board games are another item that libraries often make available for students taking a study break. Scheduled live-action games, such as tag, are also quite popular, allowing students to run wild through the stacks. By hosting regular events, from Trivial Pursuit nights, to chess, checkers, or SCRABBLE tournaments, to multiplayer Wii sports and interactive team games, libraries can draw students in and provide a much-needed dose of recreation.

Contests and Awards

Contests are another way to generate publicity, especially if you offer a remarkable prize. Many academic libraries offer the traditional "best research paper" competition, but the emergence of digital media allows for many new forms of creative and scholarly expression. A multimedia contest can definitely update the image of the library and provide materials to place on display. More and more students are gaining experience with video editing, photography, and web design, and the library could provide them with an opportunity to apply those skills. Even a simple paper airplane contest has been successful. Find ways to challenge your students and they will respond with great interest.

Awards are another way that the library can contribute to the social fabric of the campus. Various honors could be given to individuals or organizations in areas such as charity, creativity, scholarship, leadership, or cultural contributions. Awardees could be celebrated with posters or plaques that are hung in the library in a hall of fame manner. These awards could serve as an inspiration as well as a showcase for your campus community.

Class Assignments

Many class assignments involve using the resources in the library collection; however, turning the library into a case study can lead to deeper engagement. There are many ways that the library can fit into a class project: a computer science class could conceptualize your next website redesign, and engineers could brainstorm your next renovation; anthropology majors could examine how students study together, and a psychology class could explore how people feel about the library. Think beyond how students might use your collection; an academic library building or website is a great environment for multidisciplinary research and the perfect opportunity to outsource assessment or evaluation projects as part of a class assignment.

Book Groups and Film Viewings

Book groups are a natural fit for libraries. By organizing regular group meetings or facilitating an annual campuswide common book program, libraries can promote the conversational and critical-thinking aspects of reading. Similarly, films are another cornerstone of entertainment. From the campus television station to the desktop, and on mobile devices, movies are readily available to students. Libraries should not try to compete with blockbusters, but rather fulfill a niche interest such as foreign films, documentaries, independents, or cult classics. A weekly showing coupled with discussions can broaden the cultural appeal of our libraries.

Campus Programming

Most colleges have an assortment of student clubs and organizations, and many of these often seek locations for meetings or events. Offering space to them can expand the library's participation with social, artistic, and cultural experiences. This type of campus programming might include poetry slams, drama performances, speakers, lectures, training sessions, or professional activities. The library could also lend itself to student government needs, providing a central location for civic or political expression of campus concerns, ideas, and debate. These types of activities could boost the users' perceptions of the library, truly turning it into a common meeting ground for discussions, ideas, and student engagement.

Campus Media

Campus media outlets represent another valuable tool for gaining exposure. Purchasing advertisements will ensure that your message reaches a wide audience. Additionally, these media organizations, which are typically run by students, are always on the lookout for new content. If you present the library to them with an interesting angle, they will likely respond with positive coverage.

Campus Newspaper

The campus newspaper is probably the most accessible media platform available to you. In marketing terminology, *advertising* is the coverage that you pay for, while *public relations* is what they will print for free. Both of these options are viable. Libraries are filled with newsworthy content: events, displays, renovations, new databases, leisure materials, and coverage of services. Any time there is something new, be sure to send a summary to the editor. While not everything will make it into print, it is easier for the newspaper staff when concrete story ideas are submitted to them directly. To increase the chance of publication, be sure to include informative text, contact information for potential interviewees, and any related photographs.

I also recommend purchasing advertisements. Occasionally buying a one-half- or one-quarter-page ad allows you to promote several items together; this investment also indicates your support of the newspaper, potentially opening possibilities for future cooperation.

Campus Television

Campus television is another way to promote the library. These stations tend to broadcast an eclectic mix of programming, including movies, student-created shows, and college sports. Some stations play music while campus news and events scroll across the screen. When you send information to your campus newspaper, also send it to show producers to keep them informed about the library. Additionally, the library might explore sponsorship of its own weekly program, as well as the possibility of creating commercials that promote library resources and services.

Campus Radio

College radio stations also present a promotional opportunity; like television, these stations tend to offer a wide mix of programming. The majority of airtime is dedicated to music broadcasts; however, most stations air public service announcements (PSAs), which are perfect for libraries. If your station does not offer PSAs, then thirty-second advertisements are probably affordable. In addition to music, many college radio stations feature talk show segments. Keep radio staff informed about the library. Also consider the possibility of producing a weekly library-sponsored program.

College Website

Not only should your college's home page include a link to the library's site, but events and workshops should also be added to the campus calendar. If your college's website includes news feeds, videos, or photographic collections, be sure that the library is a regular contributor.

Digital Media

The Web has changed not only the way that we build and access collections, but also how we communicate. Digital media is accessible now to libraries of all sizes, since most of the software is free or inexpensive and reasonably easy to use.

Library Website

The library's website is the most valuable digital real estate that you own. With its multipurpose function, though, it can be challenging to design. Your website has to be everything to everyone: a research utility, a calendar, a guidebook, a policy manual, and a directory. Users visiting the site have a wide variety of needs, and therefore the web presence has to be flexible and accommodating. Your website should also serve as a chief promotional portal; it is a virtual billboard introducing users to new products and services. Ideally the website's messaging should progress along with the semester. Highlight computer access, printing, and other basic features during the first weeks. At midterms, advertise resources and research assistance. As finals approach, emphasize extended hours, study spaces, tutoring services, and study break events.

Other Campus Websites

Academic department websites provide another good location for library content. Customized research guides pair nicely with discipline information, and subject librarians can be matched up with each major. Additionally, course management software (e.g., Blackboard) is also an optimal space for promotional materials. Students log in to these sites to access their assignments, syllabi, and course readings, so it is only natural to embed the library into this environment.

Announcement E-mail Lists

Announcement lists are a quick way to distribute information to users. Individuals interested in receiving library news and updates can subscribe to receive periodic electronic messages; this is an opt-in process, not spam, since students are permitting us to send them informational content. Unlike the discussion lists familiar to many librarians, these announcement lists are intended to be one-way communications. Keeping the library in the user's inbox can have a positive effect; recipients are reminded of the library, and the message often sparks related questions and desire for services. E-mail lists can also be developed for specialized groups, such as resident assistants, tutors and teaching assistants, faculty, and student government leaders, permitting more customized messages.

Message Boards

Message boards provide a central forum for online discussions. These threaded conversations allow the library to solicit feedback directly from users. Students can also communicate with each other, such as setting times for study sessions or recommending books or other resources. Due to the possibility of spam, harassment, or questionable content, you might consider establishing a moderator for this channel.

Blogs

Blogs combine the features of message boards and e-mail announcement lists; new topics are regularly posted and readers are able to respond. While many libraries have ventured into the blogosphere, most of them simply use the software as a mechanism for pushing out news and forgo the conversational aspect. A key characteristic of blogs is that users can subscribe to alerts, notifying them whenever new information has been published.

Blogs have also dynamically changed how organizations share information. Instead of one person releasing content, a cross section of staff can post updates from their respective areas: circulation staff can update policies, reference librarians can share research tips, and the systems department can report database problems. Blogs allow for a more global voice of the library to be expressed.

Podcasts

While blogs, announcement lists, and message boards widen the delivery of text-based messages, podcasts do the same thing for audio content. Think of a talk-radio show developed by librarians for their user community to download; that's a podcast. Numerous academic libraries have launched these types of programs, which typically include such content as research tips, library and campus news, event and workshop announcements, guides or tours, poetry and short story readings, music, highlights of new items added to the collection, and interviews with students, faculty, and other special guests.[3] Start-up costs are relatively cheap; a quality microphone goes for about $100, the sound editing software Audacity is free, and file hosting ranges from around $10 to $15 monthly (or you can opt to upload to your own server). You can find many excellent guides to help you get started.

An inventive use of podcast technology was developed by librarians at Fairfield University (Fairfield, Connecticut); they created *Meet the Databases* to supplement their instruction efforts. This program features a librarian interviewing a persona of a popular database, who describes research content in character: Project Muse is an artist, LION is an English gentleman, and Google Scholar is a surfer.[4]

Videos

Videos are another way to reach users. Many academic libraries currently use screen-capture software to produce online tutorials and other instructional content. These video clips are helpful for walking students through databases and explaining library services. Camtasia and Captivate are the most commonly used software programs, and both offer deep academic discounts. Digital signage is another method for reaching students. Monitors placed throughout the library can be used to stream news, updates, overviews, tutorials, and other features.

Additionally, digital video cameras are available for under $150, and free editing software comes with the Microsoft and Macintosh operating systems. Videos expand the visual promotion and can include commercials for services, tours of the building, testimonials, and instructional content. The University of Virginia (Charlottesville) experimented by recruiting students to create a video to serve as an introduction to the library.[5]

I dabbled with video production myself, working with a group of students to create a syndicated program called *The Dorm,* inspired by the television show *The Office.*[6] The objective wasn't to sell the library, but rather to create a narrative that comedically reflected life at Georgia Tech. Each episode told a complete story but also featured areas on campus, highlighting services that students use. The goal was to create familiarity by relying on product placement. Videos and podcasts alike are great opportunities to create a personality for the library; they can be informative as well as entertaining.

Social Networking Sites

Social networking websites have received a lot of media attention, with Facebook and MySpace leading the way. Millions of people, many of them college students, log in to these websites daily for online social interactions. These sites are designed to connect users with a wide range of applications, and many librarians have jumped in, using the software as an outreach tool. Some of the common features of social networking websites include group calendars, message boards, e-mail, photo galleries, video and audio tools, and the ability to "friend" others. A unique feature that Facebook offers is the ability for users to build their own applications (or apps), inviting the design of customizable tools and features. The University of Michigan Libraries (Ann Arbor) developed a catalog application, as well as a JSTOR search tool. Other academic apps include note-sharing software, group project planning tools, and citation tools.

Pushing the library into social networking websites allows us to repackage our content and to present the library in a manner that is more familiar to students. By belonging to the social Web, librarians become more visible, approachable, and relatable to users. I don't recommend creating a storefront to sell library products, but rather to embed within the social network community library staff who are able to respond and promote library products as they are needed by students.

Word of Mouth

Last, but definitely not least, word of mouth is arguably the most powerful building block of your communication strategy. Despite our best efforts and all of the channels mentioned above, nothing can surpass hearing information from a friend. George Silverman provides an instructive manual on how we can develop and trigger positive word-of-mouth campaigns.[7] His central theme is that we need to move users along the decision cycle, taking them from never having heard of our products to being prospects, *triers,* adopters, and finally evangelists. In this manner we want to include word of mouth in everything that we do, by giving students good stories to tell, exceptional service, products that meet their needs, and an easy way to tell others.

Word of mouth works on two levels: expert and peer. Expert channels are formal and include professors, advisors, teaching assistants, and resident assistants. These are the official voices that advocate for how students *should* use the library. By contrast, the peer group is very informal, including friends, dorm mates, and classmates. These conversations typically reflect how students *do* use the library. It is important that we consider both avenues, since they each offer advantages. A professor encouraging students to use a particular database carries the weight of authority, while a friend raving about an easy way to get full-text articles is also quite convincing.

Another factor in this communication strategy is the difference between organic and seeded word of mouth. Organic word of mouth happens naturally, while seeded word of mouth is deliberately planted in the community. Seeding takes place by directing library advocates to spread a message or by providing faculty with content to distribute to their students. Oftentimes, seeding is used to start a buzz, but then it picks up a life of its own and grows naturally. For example, at Georgia

Tech, the Student Government Association provides thousands of day planners each fall. The library is one of the major distribution points on campus. Where we seed this information through faculty and resident assistants, news of these freebies spreads quickly, and students come to the library to grab them up quickly.

This example emphasizes the model that Silverman describes, which is that to start the first wave of word of mouth, we need to find a way of getting the product into the hands of enthusiasts and key influencers. Once they are excited about it, they will have a message to transmit, something to share with others. While many of our users might have favorable experiences, if the topic of the library never comes up during conversations, they likely won't mention it. What we need then is to make sure that we give them something to talk about, a way to keep the library on people's minds.

This is where our marketing mix comes into play. All of the building blocks work together, buttressing our entire communication effort. In the earlier example, it wasn't just the poster, the classroom demonstration, or the website that encouraged the student to try EndNote, but rather his consciousness of all of these impressions along with the assurance of his classmate. We can't view marketing as simply creating a message and sending it out to be consumed. Instead, it has to be nurtured. While our primary goal may be to increase the usage of library products, we also want to increase awareness of the marketing campaign itself; we want students sharing and talking about our advertising efforts. Maybe it is about "that funny library poster" or that "cool library video." Whatever the case, our promotions should create a buzz and reaction among the intended audience.

The way I see it, we want to intermingle practical components with spectacles. We obviously want to highlight useful elements of the library that help students be productive, yet deliver the message in an entertaining manner. This allows for useful information to be passed along naturally: content and context are united. This objective is accomplished through an ongoing series of newsworthy (or buzzworthy) actions, ideally leading students to think, "I've been hearing interesting things about the library; maybe I'll check it out."

Here are some ideas to jumpstart your brainstorming on spreading word of mouth:

One of the surest ways to get people talking is to offer an incentive. Drawings for great prizes like laptops, MP3 players, movie tickets, and other hot items are guaranteed to get noticed. However, you don't always need big-ticket prizes. Consider a promotion in your library café in which on the thirtieth of every month you randomly give away thirty cups of coffee. Or maybe you give away thirty free pages at your printer or some other small yet practical incentive.

While it is one thing to put football players on a library poster, it is another thing to invite them in to play NCAA football on an Xbox against students. While the action is under way, take photos and offer to send the pictures to participants. This creates a lasting memory, which they will likely upload to Facebook and brag about the time they tackled the star quarterback.

Everyone expects the library to have books and journals, but what about multimedia equipment? Have your library advocates and ambassadors get involved by letting them check out digital cameras, camcorders, and other equipment at the start of the semester. Frame the campaign in a way that they are documenting a week in the life of a college student, which others can follow online. As they parade around campus gathering stories, footage, and images, they can highlight the related equipment, software, workshops, and services of the library.

Art is another way to get people talking, especially if it is something unexpected. At Georgia Tech, our multimedia center was decorated with Super Mario World video game imagery over the course of a semester.[8] This art installation demonstrated the talents of our student assistants, the capabilities of our software and printers, and a more humorous and lighthearted side of the library. Students working on assignments in this space were surrounded by the artwork and felt like they were actually within the game world. Now, many semesters later, students still talk about this display and wonder what's next.

Your circulation desk probably has hundreds of transactions a day; this is a great touch point with users. While they are checking out items, library staff can briefly mention a particular product or service (e.g., a new database, the library instant messenger account, an upcoming event, or the DVD collection), potentially opening a conversation with the user. Interested students can be encouraged to take a flier with additional information. The content delivered through this channel could change weekly corresponding with ongoing campaigns.

Many of us have dabbled with the librarian-on-location model, in which a librarian takes a laptop and sets up shop in the student center, a classroom building, or a dorm in hopes of reaching passersby. Another approach might be to target specific dorms and work with housing offices and resident assistants to drum up business. Host a regular weekly session, let's say Wednesday evenings from five to six, when a librarian is available to help. You can then target this with a wide marketing mix, and especially with word of mouth, to generate a buzz within that dorm. The housing office might also contribute snacks; often they have a budget for academic support events. Along with spontaneous visits, you also get people who plan to attend. Be sure to emphasize *research help,* rather than *librarian* in your promotions.

Probably the simplest way generate word of mouth is to ask for it. Whenever you encounter a student who is grateful, ask him or her to share the experience with friends and classmates.

As we shape our communication strategy, it's important to seed some form of word of mouth. As we plan our posters, fliers, and newspaper and web coverage, we should also conceptualize the channels through which this type of information will spread. We want to make it as easy, exciting, and valuable as possible for students to share with each other. Once we open the door by giving them something to talk about, their other library experiences will funnel into the conversation.

THE MESSAGE, NOT THE MEDIUM

Getting the attention of your users is relatively easy, but turning that awareness into results is the real challenge. You have an abundance of promotional tools at your disposal; however, flooding the campus with information is not necessarily the most effective strategy. We need our communication efforts to be organized, concise, and on target. In the next chapter we'll examine the process of designing messages and making sure that your content is reaching the right people, at the right time, in the right place, and in the right format.

NOTES

1. Brian Mathews and Jon Bodnar, *Promoting the Library, SPEC Kit 306* (Washington, DC: Association of Research Libraries, 2008).
2. Brian Mathews, "Chicken Wings and Egg Rolls: The Library Menu Concept," *The Ubiquitous Librarian* blog, http://theubiquitouslibrarian.typepad.com/the_ubiquitous_librarian/2007/05/chicken_wings_a.html.
3. Meredith Farkas, "Podcasting," in *Library Success: A Best Practices Wiki,* www.libsuccess.org/index.php?title=Podcasting.
4. DiMenna-Nyselius Library, Fairfield University, "Meet the Databases!" www.fairfield.edu/lib_podcasts.html.
5. University of Virginia Libraries, *Libra Video,* www.lib.virginia.edu/student_video/libravideo.html and www.apple.com/education/profiles/virginia/index2.html.
6. Georgia Tech students, "The Dorm," www.youtube.com/user/WatchTheDorm.
7. George Silverman, *The Secrets of Word-of-Mouth Marketing: How to Trigger Exponential Sales through Runaway Word of Mouth* (New York: AMACOM, 2001).
8. Brian Mathews, "Super Mario Multimedia World: An Art Installation in the Georgia Tech Library," *The Ubiquitous Librarian* blog, http://theubiquitouslibrarian.typepad.com/the_ubiquitous_librarian/2007/01/super_mario_mul.html.

9

Designing Messages

Promoting the library can be a lot of fun; it allows you to be creative, and it is extremely satisfying when you receive a positive response to your endeavors. However, effective marketing is not happenstance; it is planned. Each of the promotional building blocks discussed in the previous chapter serves as a separate ingredient that, when combined, form a complete meal. When designing your message, think of it as a series of dishes, each requiring different ingredients in varying amounts, mixed together at different times. Similar to preparing a gourmet feast with each course complementing another, you want to spread out your promotional messages across the entire semester. Finding the right marketing mix is challenging, but with proper planning you can optimize your efforts. This chapter serves as your recipe for designing messages that will reach students. We'll look at tone, objectives, location, timing, and attributes.

COMMON LIBRARY CAMPAIGNS

I edited a SPEC Kit for the Association of Research Libraries on the topic of library promotions, and I have to confess that it was an eye-opening experience.[1] Among the survey participants there was much variety in staffing, budgets, and production quality, but one common theme: the iconic image of the term paper. Libraries often depicted the process of conducting research as a struggle, with students stressed out by trying to find appropriate resources. In the sample of promotional materials, librarians were regularly presented as heroes, guiding users through this difficult ordeal, and subscription databases were represented as super tools enabling students to locate appropriate information.

Personally I feel this message is off the mark. While locating and obtaining resources can indeed be a challenge, students shared with me that it is synthesizing the information that is most difficult: putting the pieces together, presenting the evidence, forming the argument, and writing the paper—not necessarily the act of searching or citing articles. The tone of our advertisements illustrates a fundamental problem in the way that academic libraries communicate with undergraduates: we talk down to them. While this arrogance may be unintentional, focus group testing of these types of messages reveals a negative response from students. Many users have indicated that they find this language to be condescending, irrelevant, humorless, and even deterring.

This response should not be taken too lightly; our promotional materials might actually be turning people away from the library. How did we end up so out of touch with our intended audience? Perhaps our perceptions of students are shaped too heavily by reference or circulation desk transactions. If this is the case, then the theme of desperation is understandable; however, portraying research as a struggle may actually be harmful to our effort. We belittle our students by positioning ourselves as missionaries charged with converting everyone into expert users. My concern, from a marketing standpoint, is that we may be reflecting our own interpretation of the value of libraries and librarians, presenting ourselves as crusaders or protectors of the noble pursuit of knowledge. When you are planning a campaign, think carefully about how you represent the library. Be sure that the image you project is authentic and relatable to your students.

INSPIRATION: A NEW MESSAGE

Instead of a parental message touting that *we know best,* library promotions should be inspiring. Instead of simply peddling our wares, why not strive to motivate students, giving them encouragement and confidence? If we want to make a splash, we have to move beyond the *term paper blues* and showcase the wide array of products and services that we offer. By expanding our message and more clearly defining the function of the library, we can craft a more engaging image, resulting in increased usage and positive word of mouth.

Aside from appealing to students on a purely functional level, we can leverage emotional appeals as well. This is where the brand strategy from chapter 7 comes into play. Consider how carmakers advertise their automobiles: not only do they mention miles per gallon, speed, and reliability, but they also tap into emotional attributes such as prestige, patriotism, pleasure, safety, and environmental concerns. For many people owning a car is more than just driving a vehicle; it is a personal bond that is representative of who they are. Likewise, how people feel about the library can have an impact on their usage as well as their openness to learning more.

Consider an emotional appeal when designing messages. Focus on the psychological benefits and motivational triggers, as opposed to a purely factual statement. Quiet study is about escapism. Group study is about social learning. Librarians are troubleshooters. Instead of dumbing down the library, we can elevate our message by associating ourselves with academic, cultural, social, technological, and other accomplishments. Here are a few examples of broad-ranged campaigns that set a more positive and customer-sensitive tone:

The lifestyle of the user. Show how the library is an everyday stop: from printing to studying, to film viewings, to lunch, and so forth. The library offers something for everyone; it is both a social and academic destination. This message reveals value through the users' interactions.

Connections. Demonstrate the interconnectedness of the library: how it brings people, technology, and ideas together. Show how resources, disciplines, and various services all share common threads.

The library is more than you imagine. Students arrive on campus with assumptions about the library, so surprise them by showing that it is more than what they thought it was. Emphasize the depth of your product inventory and expand their idea of what the library is all about.

OBJECTIVES

Objectives are what we *hope* will happen; they are the desired impact of our marketing. Once your message is released on campus, what are the results? What actions do you anticipate students taking after encountering your material? What do you consider a success and what is a failure? In chapter 10 we'll tackle the evaluation of our promotional efforts in great detail, but keep your goals in mind when developing a communication strategy. Whether your intentions are to reach a highly specialized group or a very broad audience, you will most likely seek one of these following objectives:

Objective 1: Attracting new users. Most academic libraries place an emphasis on outreach. We cannot just wait around for users to contact us; we must take proactive measures in an effort to make students aware of library products and services. Classrooms, course management systems, computer labs, orientations, dorms, and cafés are prime opportunities to reach the uninitiated. The objective of this type of campaign is to introduce nonusers, infrequent users, or new students to the library.

Objective 2: Attendance. Event-driven advertising is another common objective. Academic libraries host a wide array of programming including classes, workshops, tutoring, film viewings, exhibits, special lectures, and social activities. The objective of this type of campaign is to bring people in, whether for a onetime event or as part of a series. Often, the lure of entertainment can spark interest in additional library services. Get them in and let them see what else you have to offer.

Objective 3: Use of products. Awareness of library products is another frequent objective. Getting the word out about virtual reference, group study rooms, or JSTOR can help the library connect with students by focusing on their specific needs. Emotional and functional attributes come into play because you not only want to present the facts, but offer motivational enticement as well. The goal with this type of campaign is to pique the user's interest, resulting in a trial of the product.

Objective 4: Perception of the library. While the other three objectives focus on the more tangible values of the library, another possibility is to build reputation, or the library's brand. What is the character of the building? Is it welcoming or is it sterile? Is it a place where students want to be or a place that they have to be? Is it a student-centered or a library-centered organization? This form of advertising aims to make a connection with the user; it is driven by symbolism, attitude, and spirit. The goal isn't necessarily to promote a particular service or resource, but rather to be entertaining, thought-provoking, or amusing. The objective is to change or enhance the perceptions of students, giving the library a richer identity and personality.

Of course many campaigns will interweave several of these objectives. For example, you may create a promotional package directed toward transfer students with the hope of introducing them to the library. This effort could include a series of academic and social events, as well as information about specific tools and resources. Additionally, this campaign might hit an emotional chord, welcoming them in and positioning the library to help their transition into the school. By bringing together a group of transfer students, allowing them to meet each other, and providing a personalized library orientation, you may foster a positive bonding experience between them and your organization.

LOCATION

Another important component that factors into the design of a successful marketing campaign is location. "Location, location, location" is the battle cry of retailers and real estate agents across the world, and we can learn a lot from them. Obviously, if students do not encounter our promotional materials, then we cannot expect them to react to them, so it is imperative that those materials are in their line of sight. We need to be sure that our advertising makes an impression. However, simply plastering the campus with fliers is not necessarily the best strategy. Instead, we want to focus on appropriate placements that ensure relevant and repeated viewings.

The most obvious location for our promotional material is in the library building itself. Many students visit our facilities regularly, but the majority of them are unaware of all of the products that we have to offer. Consider the many surfaces in the library available to us for distributing messages: elevators, hallways, bathrooms, display cases, tables and cubicles, entranceways, exterior walls, computer clusters, lounge areas, cafés, monitors or digital signage, and public service desks. In fact, every space in the library is a potential billboard; however, the danger exists of overexposure. Too much advertising will result in an unattractive, cluttered, and confusing Times Square type of environment, where all of the messages blend together and are collectively ignored. Yet with the right balance and by keeping the material refreshed, the library building becomes our greatest promotional tool.

While the library is a logical location, many other spots on campus are also effective. Dorms, dining halls, the student center, and bus stops are high-density places. Other units on campus are typically willing to work with library staff and have set policies and procedures for advertising. Be sure to follow these; otherwise your work may be removed. Classrooms and computer labs are also ideal; during a course lecture, a wandering eye might happen upon your poster, leaving a memorable impression and a welcome distraction. Chalking is another possible option. Many students have told me that they find out about campus events and other information through chalk drawings and messages scrawled temporarily on high-traffic walkways.

These locations can be virtual as well. The library website is a great channel for promoting your vast product inventory; banner ads, featured spotlights, videos, blogs, chat sessions, and photos are some of the tools that can be used to showcase services and resources. However, not all students will come across the library's site, and many who do might tune out or overlook the advertising, so a presence in other online destinations is indispensable. Another valuable plot of virtual real estate is in your school's course management system. Packaging library information alongside course assignments and the syllabus will definitely get your material noticed. Additionally, gaining the endorsement of a professor increases credibility and improves the odds that students will actually pay attention to your content. In this manner, the library becomes part of the classroom instead of a supplemental service.

While the course management system offers a formal connection to students, social websites present an opportunity to develop a more informal relationship. Students are using Facebook, blogs, Flickr, Twitter, and similar sites to interact with each other, and librarians can use these windows to join the conversation. Social web tools enable us to disseminate information and interact with library users in ways that were previously unavailable. By designing library-themed groups, maintaining personal profiles, and engaging students in this digital environment, we can extend the bounds of our advocacy.

As you plan your campaign, take advantage of the expressive characteristics of these various locations. Instead of simply printing hundreds of fliers and plastering them around campus, customize the material for different places: colorful posters in the library, funky fliers distributed in the dorms, a humorous video for the Web, a surprising ad in the school newspaper, or a tutorial uploaded onto Blackboard. Just as commercial content varies on TV, radio, and print, you should adapt your message accordingly. Items designed for the dorm should have a different tone than material created for use in the library or the classroom. Consider the mindset of the student at the time and place that they encounter your message. For example, if I intend to use table tents in a student dining hall, then I want to be sure to look at what's currently in place. I take note of the attitude or spirit of the environment; dining halls tend to be lively, loud, and filled with jokes and humor. I want to make sure that my message fits in appropriately. I may even take a few prototypes with me and gather initial feedback from my target audience. Spending just ten minutes talking with students can be the difference between a huge success and a total flop.

TIMING

Timing is everything! Developing a great message and placing it in a suitable location will only work if the timing is right, too. I have found that each semester generally comprises three stages. Developing your promotional campaign to unfold across each of these phases will greatly improve your chances for relevancy. Let's look at each one:

STAGE 1
The Orientation Period (Weeks 1–4)

During the initial weeks of each semester, students are generally upbeat and optimistic about the months ahead. Of course they feel some stress and nervous anticipation, especially if they are freshmen adjusting to a major lifestyle change, but overall this period is marked by positive emotion. Students start with a clean slate and are not yet buried with academic pressures. They tend to be less busy and more open to a wide range of activities. This is the ideal time for welcoming or social events.

Your message during this phase should focus on the broad perception of the library: a simple introduction. Anything too serious or detailed will be ignored. Instead, try to draw attention to the library brand or a core idea that matches their mindset. Highlight something about the library that is unusual or unexpected, draw them in with intrigue, and make them curious. This is a casual time requiring a casual tone. The library may not be the most exciting place on campus, but it is safe, friendly, and inviting, and there is always something going on. Possible content themes include

Individuals. Present the library as a destination between classes: a place to check e-mail, grab a coffee, read a magazine, or print out class notes. Demonstrate how the library fits naturally into the flow of the school day.

Group work. Show a group of friends hanging out in the library. They should be involved in some type of action such as scanning or photocopying notes, eating in the café, or attending an event. Position the library as a gathering place that is both social and functional in nature.

Technology. Highlight your library commons or computer lab. A simple artistic photo with basic information is all that is necessary. Pique their interest to come and check it out. The point to get across is that the library has robust technology in a comfortable modern environment.

Collections. While it is tempting to impress students with the size of print collections or the number of full-text databases available, hold off on that for now. Instead, highlight the DVD collection or leisure books and magazines. Students expect their academic library to have expansive scholarly collections, so entice them with something fun or unexpected.

STAGE 2
The Productivity Period (Weeks 5–11)

During this phase students encounter tests, midterms, and an assortment of readings and assignments. Each week requires them to ramp up their academic output. The shiny wrapper of the semester has worn off, and students shift into a period of serious work. This is our opportunity to highlight specific products and tools that students can use. In stage 1 the goal was to create a generally positive feeling toward the library; in this phase we move more toward demonstrating what we have to offer. The central theme here is *getting things done.* The library is a bridge between the classroom and the dorm room: a laboratory for study, schoolwork, and ideas. It is a place to go to be productive. It is a tool kit—a suite of services collected and designed to achieve success. Amid this academic focus are small pockets of downtime and relaxation.

The occasional game night or cultural event can be an outlet for stress relief, providing a much-needed distraction. During this stage we want to continue building their connection with the library. Possible content themes include:

Individuals. Highlight the variety of study spaces in the library: some are quiet, some are noisy, some are tucked away in the stacks, and others are comfortable and out in the open. Position the library as flexible and accommodating, with a wide range of areas designed for different types of study and productivity. Illustrate that the library has a place for everyone.

Group work. Similar to individual spaces, highlight areas designated for group work. If you have study rooms, show how they are used with concise descriptions of policy and procedures. If you have group computing or a collaborative area, show students working together. Paint a picture of the library as a team-friendly environment, loaded with all the tools, technology, spaces, supplies, services, furniture, and people that they need.

Technology. Highlight the software available on library computers. This could include Microsoft Office and other tools such as SPSS or Photoshop. Additionally, point out any gadgets that are available for checkout such as webcams, video recorders, or digital cameras. These could be useful as part of a class project, as well as for personal interest. Showcasing your technology continues to position the library as an intriguingly modern and diverse facility.

Collections. This is the time to talk about resources. Students expect the library to have mountains of information, so let them see what you have to offer. Databases should be woven into your message: position them as tools designed for the assignments that they are working on. Also highlight full-text and remote access. I recommend both a broad message emphasizing the wide range of research materials, as well as targeted communications directed at specific disciplines or courses.

STAGE 3
The Closing Period (Weeks 12–16)

Welcome to crunch time: students are finishing up assignments, rehearsing presentations, and preparing for exams. The final weeks of each semester are fascinating; this is when many students seem to come out of the woodwork and discover the library. Each passing week delivers a mounting chaos that culminates with finals. Personal time is scarce, and students are typically determined, focused, and perhaps a touch scatterbrained.

Your promotional message during this period should continue the theme of productivity, but should be fully aligned with functional attributes. While they need the various services, spaces, and resources of the library, they also need encouragement. Students are under a lot of pressure, and a little empathy can go a long way in our cause. Position the library as a support system; focus on their success and follow-through during the semester. This is when students need help from tutors and teaching assistants, writing center staff, librarians, and peers. Convenience, efficiency, and motivation are some key characteristics during this phase; don't talk down to them, but rather talk them up and build their confidence. Possible content themes include

Individuals. "Space to spread out" is a central image that you want to portray. Show that the library is accommodating, open late, and the perfect place to get away from the distractions of the dorm. With comfortable furniture, food, and all the necessary supplies, the library is *home* for the final weeks.

Group work. Group activity will intensify as the semester progresses. At this point you want to put their mounting energy and concentration on display. If you have an area where many groups typically gather, highlight the mass of people in the library. Demonstrate that it is not just a sleepy building, but a dynamic atmosphere: one group is practicing for a presentation, another working on calculus problems, another quizzing each other with note cards, another eating pizza, and so forth. Plant the idea that this is the place where groups want to meet and where they get work done.

Technology. Due to the fact that many students who don't frequently use the library will be dropping in, make computer usage easy and intuitive for them. With advertising, stick to the basics: printing and programs. Students will be tilted toward academic work, so focus on meeting those core needs. Libraries can be intimidating, especially when others around them seem to understand how everything works, so place an emphasis on policy, procedure, and productivity.

Collections. During crunch time, full text is the student's best friend. While a good portion of our job is curating scholarly collections, undergraduates operating under a deadline simply need adequate material. Finding several articles on the crisis of health care, immigration, or terrorism should not be an epic battle. Instead, emphasize the convenience, broad scope, credibility, and instant access that library resources can provide.

Consider how your message can evolve across the semester. The way you pitch the learning commons in week three is different than in week thirteen. The attitude and personality of your communications should evolve along with the changing needs and outlook of your students. Be sure to demonstrate the functional value of the library, but also try to connect with them on an emotional level. Present the library as a package of services that is exactly what they need at the time they need it.

ATTRIBUTES OF A STORY

Advertising is like telling a good story. You need a hook to draw people in. Once they are invested, a compelling plot will keep them interested, and the end should be a satisfying conclusion. That is the basic framework that I use when developing a promotional campaign. When looking at a particular library service or resource, I consider what makes it most desirable. Who are the ideal users? What does it help them accomplish? And when are they most likely to use the product? Once these basics are established (who, what, when, and where), the narrative begins falling into place. When the facts are set, then you can work on the more subjective and insightful questions: how and why. What motivates someone to use these services, and what is the end result? It is one thing to say that you have subject experts who can help with research questions twenty-four hours a day via online chat. But it is a more persuasive story to show how students use the service: the girl who texted a librarian for citation information while in class, or the guy who got help at three in the morning in his dorm room. It's the narrative that draws people in. I suggest creating several storyboards of how different students use the product that you want to promote. Your message will emerge from this exercise.

Along with telling a story, there are numerous characteristics that you can use to present content.[2] In every campaign I try to use aspects that are surprising, relatable, tangible, experiential, shareable, and measurable.

While undoubtedly there are many other important elements, these six attributes provide a foundation for effectively reaching college students:

Surprising

In a world cluttered with commercial noise, the library has to work hard to break through and get noticed. The root of gaining attention is to present the unexpected, something unanticipated that breaks the usual patterns to which students are accustomed. Such features could be creative or imaginative artwork, concepts, or text; however, there has to be substance attached as well. A humorous or shocking photo might succeed in gaining awareness, but if the content doesn't adhere, then your message will get lost.

This notion of *surprising the user* is befitting of libraries. Students are typically so entrenched in traditional stereotypes that breaking their assumptions can be to our advantage. This process of extending their perceptions works in our favor because the library becomes an ongoing story: a narrative in which our product lines continuously unfold. When we appeal to students' sense of curiosity, they will begin to wonder what's next, or what else there is.

Can you conjure an intriguing sensation or a sense of mystery? Keep this in mind when brainstorming. I like to involve students in a media approach because you can focus on their journey, allowing others to discover the library along with them. This method attempts to create enduring interest in which students want to know what happens next or how it will end. *What happened to the guy asking a reference question at three in the morning?* Another classic tactic is to highlight a gap in a person's knowledge. The realization that he doesn't know something fuels his curiosity, so pose questions, puzzles, or challenges that incite a natural sense of inquiry. *How many books can you check out?*

We can present students lots of facts and useful information, but unless they want to receive it, our efforts may be fruitless. A large part of what advertising is about is convincing people they need to know more. Use the element of surprise to grab their attention and then surprise them even further with a valuable message.

Relatable

Developing a message that students inherently understand is absolutely vital. This doesn't mean just using a student spokesperson or clever wordplay on some college slang. The information you present has to be relevant; it has to be something that students care about. We need to deliver the content in an appropriate context that makes sense to the user. I've seen several library campaigns mimicking television programs or commercials, hoping the popularity will rub off, but we have to beware of undermining the intention. We shouldn't blatantly rip off hit shows and expect students to perceive the library as cool. We have to be authentic, speaking in our own voice. While it is OK to *borrow* some familiar motifs, we don't want to distract from the integrity of the message.

Library advertising should be squarely focused on the users: students are the stars, not the library or librarians. We have to appeal to their sense of self-interest. Successful promotions do not rely on smoke and mirrors, but rather demonstrate how library products enhance the student's life. Your communications should be layered with inspiration and incentive; they should make people want to use the library because it fits particular needs at a particular time. Our goal is to present the library as an intuitive and obvious choice.

Tangible

Every campaign should feature a tactile component—an element that users can feel, fold, save, and take with them. Simply hanging a poster, even a well-designed one, will probably only capture fleeting interest. However, supplemental fliers, coupons, photos, handouts, or other giveaways can serve as a reminder. College students are on the go, so while a poster might pique their interest, they need an object that they can turn to later. Think of this as developing a portable communication strategy; implant your message on something tangible that students can carry with them. Digital objects work well, too: a photo, PDF document, audio file, or video clip. The objective is to put your message in their hands, or on their desktop, so that it is available at an opportune time.

Experiential

Your message should also feature an interactive component. Images and text can describe a service, but users who experience something can gain a lasting impression. Some of the most effective promotional campaigns are those that prompt viewers to action, such as visiting a website, playing a game, solving a puzzle, completing a story line, creating customized content, or interacting with others. Try infusing a participatory element into your design as an effort to encourage response.

Shareable

Word of mouth is an attribute that we want to try and harness. While most word of mouth happens naturally, our goal is to get people talking about the library. This can be done by using qualities that are entertaining, novel, or cool. Aside from an intriguing design, your communication strategy should also highlight library products that students are inherently interested in, such as a DVD collection or gadgets and technology. This can produce the desired social effect of encouraging students to mention the library naturally in conversations. Additionally, activities such as gaming nights or guest speakers as well as unusual events, art, or displays can draw students in, possibly bringing friends along with them. Practical applications will also garner attention with students recommending databases, study spaces, and other useful items to their peers. Their discussions may cover procedural aspects such as finding books or how to print. Many students learn about the library from other students; therefore, we need to consider the social properties during our planning phase to be sure we make our messages accommodating. Our goal should be to give users something to talk about, affording them the opportunity and desire to share our content.

Measurable

You should always attempt to build assessment into everything you do. This may not always be possible, especially for intangible qualities such as retention or inspiration, but you will want to know if your effort is paying off. For our purposes, measurability falls into two categories: (1) the effectiveness of the promotional material and (2) the impact the promotional material had on services. You are investing time and money on developing a message, so be sure to complete the circle and gather feedback from the audience. Did they like it? Did they hate it? Did they even notice it? How could it be improved? Was it timely? Was it informative? These answers will help you improve future efforts, so find ways to build in assessment. Secondly, and perhaps most important, you want to know your return on investment: did your advertising work? One of the simplest ways to derive success is by having a call-to-action component built into the design, such as attending an event, filling out a form, or visiting a website. Requiring some type of measurable response enables you to determine the reach of your marketing effort. We'll look into measuring the impact more thoroughly in chapter 10.

You may not always be able to include all six of these attributes in your messaging. Sometimes you may not need to; a simple flier or classroom demonstration might be enough. It all depends on what you are trying to project and who you're trying to reach. However, these characteristics, along with the other components outlined in this chapter, serve as guideposts that you can use to construct a fully developed message.

Marketing is an endless cycle. We are constantly admitting new students, and with them a new chance to make a strong impression. More than anything else, I want to impress upon you this opportunity to experiment with communication techniques. Marketing is something we learn only through continued experiences.

NOTES

1. Brian Mathews and Jon Bodnar, *Promoting the Library, SPEC Kit 306* (Washington, DC: Association of Research Libraries, 2008).
2. Chip Heath and Dan Heath, *Made to Stick: Why Some Ideas Survive and Others Die* (New York: Random House, 2007).

10 Measuring the Impact

An enduring reflection by marketing legend John Wanamaker made in the early years of the twentieth century states that half the money spent on advertising is wasted; the trouble is that executives don't know which half that is. This problem still persists today. A recent study of major corporate campaigns reports that one-third of promotional material is ineffective.[1] Accountability is a growing issue in the industry, and likewise it is a concern for librarians because we need to know, does it work? With budget fluctuations and competing priorities, library administrators want to be sure that our efforts have an impact. Costs for food, events, giveaways, and printing add up quickly, and managers want a good return on their investment. Frontline staff also have a keen interest in outcomes, wanting to optimize their outreach efforts and ensure that students learn about services and resources.

While it may seem obvious that assessment is an important step in the communication process, most academic libraries don't do it. My study for the Association of Research Libraries found that less than 30 percent of the participants evaluated their promotional campaigns.[2] Those who did typically relied on single methods or anecdotal evidence. This chapter tackles the challenge of measuring the impact of our promotional efforts. We'll look at several techniques that you can apply to your marketing program.

METRICS

When it comes to marketing, there is no shortage of metrics.[3] The difference that we face as librarians is that we do not run businesses; we do not generate profit through sales and therefore cannot link consumer behavior to the current advertising push. Student motivation is a sticky area. It is hard to pin down exactly why someone uses a particular service. Libraries, after all, are a campus utility, and whether we advertise or not, some students will find their way through our doors or onto our website. Assignments are another factor; if students need to locate information or require a quiet place to study, the library is a logical option. Although our promotions may serve to increase awareness, we cannot necessarily take credit for something that is inherent. Many factors can lead to library use, and we have to take that into account as we develop our messages. But we also need to factor in some level of accountability and test the impact of our efforts. The following methods are ideal for academic libraries.

Response-Based Advertising

One of the easiest ways to gauge the reach of advertising is by involving a response. This is commonly referred to as a *call to action* in which the customer is asked to respond directly to a marketing message. You have probably seen this before in television commercials or magazine ads where people are encouraged to visit a website, call a toll-free number, or take advantage of a limited time offer. Not only does this engage the would-be customer, but it gives the marketer a chance to track how people saw the advertisement. If a grocery store mails out coupons, they can measure effectiveness by seeing how many customers took advantage of the discount.

Directing people to a website is probably the simplest way to get a response. Instead of guiding students to your home page, create a campaign-specific secondary page that allows you to keep web statistics. These special pages could be set up for library events, information on equipment or supplies, databases or collections, as well as instructional content. Let's look at how this might work. Say that your library offers a monthly lecture series, bringing in a professor, community member, or other guest speaker to talk about a timely topic. You create a website dedicated to this program that includes biographical information, upcoming presenters, and recordings of past speakers. Three weeks before the next event, you hang a poster around the library and in the student center announcing a distinguished author who will be visiting campus. This promo poster will direct students to the website, which you can track to see if there is any early interest. The following week you purchase a half-page ad in the school paper and also send out information to faculty and campus leaders, encouraging them to share the announcement with students. Again, the URL becomes part of the message. Finally, a week before the event, you distribute fliers around campus and at the circulation desk and add a banner ad to your library's home page. By scattering your promotional activities over time you can observe the reaction caused by each different channel. This lets you see what worked best.

Another way to measure impact is by promoting specific tools or services. If you run a campuswide campaign pushing your chat reference service and you notice that numbers double over the semester, then this is a strong indication that the advertising worked. Any time that you can have students do something, such as fill out a form, ask a question, click on a link, watch a video, attend an event, or participate in a contest, it serves as a way to quantify the reaction to the campaign.

Market Share

Another concept that we can borrow from the business world is market share. This indicator is calculated by counting the total number of users, subscribers, or customers and dividing that by the total population. For example, a company may look at their figures in a modest-sized city and see that they sold their product to five thousand households. The total population is one hundred thousand households, making their market share 5 percent. This metric creates a baseline for the particular community, allowing the company to compare this number with other towns and cities across the nation. They can also boost advertising through commercials, newspaper ads, free samples, and special displays in retail outlets. After several months of new promotions they can crunch the numbers again to see if their market share has increased.

Libraries might not have sales data, but there are several transactions that we can use as benchmarks. By analyzing unique log-ins to computers over the duration of a semester, we can find out how many students used the library. Let's say that the undergraduate population at your school is ten thousand and that your unique undergraduate log-ins for the fall semester were forty-five hundred. This would mean that your market share or the number of students who logged in at least once would be 45 percent, or slightly less than half of all students enrolled. As an attempt to increase usage, maybe you launch a campaign that prominently features your library commons. At the end of the spring term you could review your data again to see if the advertising worked based on an increase to your market share.

The same concept can be applied to databases, circulation statistics, and other areas as well. How many unique remote users log in to the proxy? How many students checked out a book? While academic libraries commonly report their total annual circulation numbers, they don't typically calculate their market share. Again, if your student population is ten thousand and one hundred thousand items circulate, then we can't assume that every person checked out a book. Digging into the data might reveal that there were actually four thousand individuals who borrowed at least one item over the course of the year. This would indicate a market share of 40 percent. As marketers we would be drawn to the 60 percent of the population who didn't check out materials and would see if we could possibly increase transactions.

This strategy could also be applied to different user segments. What percentage of freshmen visited the library in their first semester? How many students in a particular class used our resources? How many chairs, desks, or computers are typically occupied throughout the day? What I like about market share is that it helps us determine the amount of use, as well as the nonusage of our products. This gives us measurable goals that we can try to improve upon.

How Did You Hear about This?

Sometimes the best way to find out if your advertising was effective is to simply ask, how did you hear about this? Students who use a particular product or service can be invited to share their experience. Prompt them for their discovery process: where did they hear about the lecture series, or how did they find out about the digital cameras at circulation? Build these types of questions into the regular delivery of services. Even if this is an informal process, soliciting this type of information can help you track down how students find out about the library's offerings.

A variation of this strategy is to send users a follow-up e-mail. While there are certainly advantages to talking with students directly after they used a product, contacting them a week or two later lets them respond on their own time. A student who reserves a group study room, checks out a laptop, attends an event, or e-mails a reference question can opt in to receive an exit survey about their library transaction. This method of directly asking users can yield vast results, from how they heard about the service to their thoughts, opinions, suggestions, satisfaction, or problems they encountered. We can also ask for their advice on how we should tell other students about the particular service.

Web Analytics

The library website is another window into user behavior. Online traffic patterns not only tell us what students are looking for, but what they find or don't find and what they end up using. Two of the most common web advertising metrics are total hits and click-through rates. Let's say that your home page averages four thousand unique visitors each day. If you placed a promotional message on the site, a banner ad, a blog post, a spotlight, or some other prominent link, you can assume that four thousand people viewed it. Of course not everyone will notice it, but placing information on the home page increases the odds. Traditional marketing aims for volume: the more eyes the better, because a large audience means greater exposure of the message.

While hit counts allow us to keep track of how many people are visiting our site, click-through rates provide more details. This strategy lets us gauge the effectiveness, or at least the appeal, of our messages. Continuing the example above, if you placed a notice on your home page about an upcoming event and five hundred people clicked on it during the day, your rate would be 13 percent. This number indicates the number of daily visitors who opted to learn more about the speaker. Click-throughs provide us with a more reliable and realistic estimate of how many people actually see our ads. It lets us know the types of content or images that get people's attention.

You can also use advertising on your website as a means of engaging users and influencing their behavior. The Western Michigan University Libraries (Kalamazoo) demonstrate this by creating banner ads that prompt actions on behalf of the user, such as recommending DVDs to be added to the collection or reminding students to renew their books.[4] Analyzing their data, they found that click-throughs led to positive results and generated more awareness, circulation, and suggestions for DVDs, as well as an overall increase in online book renewals. By encouraging measurable interactions we can correlate the relationship between our advertising and library usage.

I highly recommend Google Analytics.[5] This free and relatively easy-to-use software provides you with a powerful suite of website measurement. The Analytics tool allows you to track and discover information about your users, including what pages they visit, how frequently they access them, how long they stay, what they click on, and where they give up. This detailed analysis not only aids your marketing effort, but can also help your library improve its web design. See figure 10.1 for a sample of the data that can be collected.

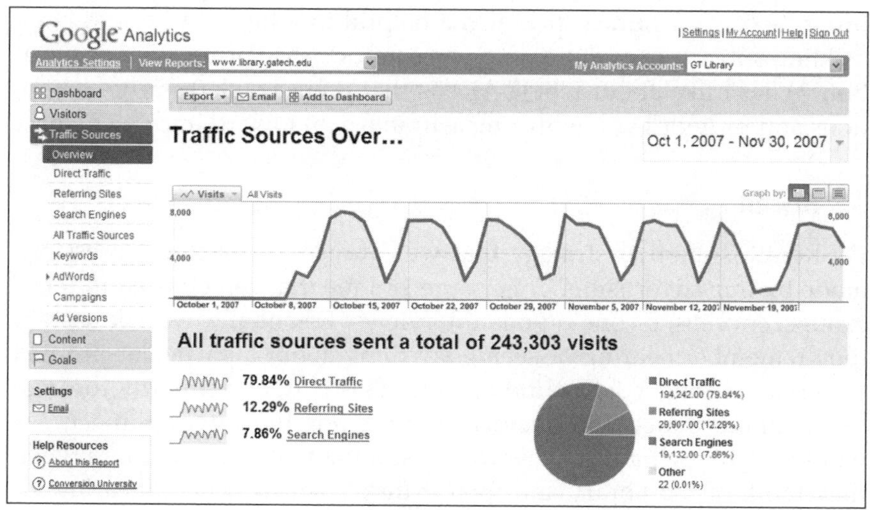

FIGURE 10.1
Google Analytics sample data

LibQUAL+

LibQUAL+ is one of the best all-around tools that you can have in your assessment portfolio. It is like a report card for your library. In chapter 5, I offered suggestions on using this national survey for conducting marketing research, but LibQUAL+ can also let you know if marketing works. One of the strengths of this assessment tool is that it lets you carve up your population by disciplines, enabling you to distinguish any unique perspectives. Are business majors dissatisfied with e-resources? Do engineers want more group study space? LibQUAL+ allows us to know the broad areas that require immediate attention; it also lets us know if an ongoing campaign is working. If you are strongly pushing full-text journals through numerous channels, low survey results would suggest that your message is not getting through.

LibQUAL+ is also great for longitudinal analysis. The first time you participate in the survey you get a snapshot of user perceptions. If you implement the survey a few years later, you can see how opinions have evolved over time. Fluctuations could be a reaction to any changes that you've made to services or spaces, as well as a reflection on your marketing. If you notice that students are dissatisfied with group study space, you can address this through your communication efforts. In this regard, LibQUAL+ serves as a benchmark, allowing you to monitor the progress of your library. It is also a helpful tool for brand assessment, tackling subjective qualities such as comfort, ease of use, and inspiration. What I like about LibQUAL+ is that it encapsulates user perceptions and provides you with a measurable goal toward improvement.

Recall

Recall is another strategy that we can use to test the impressions made by our advertising. This is a technique that can be used in focus groups, surveys, or one-on-one interviews. Essentially, we ask users if they remember hearing or seeing anything about a particular product or service during a set period of time. This is done primarily through two methods: aided and unaided recall. Using the latter approach, we would ask participants to share the first thing that comes to mind when they think of the library and then if they recollect seeing, hearing, or reading about any of our services. This is referred to as unaided because users draw on their memories and experiences, rather than on what we supply them. Aided recall is different in that we specifically ask users for their impression about a particular service. Did they encounter any information about guest speakers, group study rooms, or reference assistance over the past semester? We could also place a poster, flier, handout, or other promotional piece in front of them and ask if they remember seeing it.

Recall is a direct way for us to find out how students discover information about various library products. We can give them a floor plan of the library and have them indicate which areas they have used. This exercise can help initiate discussions about spaces, resources, and services and help us try to assess our promotional efforts. We could also give students a list of databases and ask them to circle any they have used, as well as have them walk us through the library website, sharing links and tools that they have used in the past. This undertaking would be especially helpful to test ongoing outreach, for example, to see if biology majors are familiar with key databases, subject guides, or their subject librarian. In this manner, recall is insightful for measuring the reach of our advertising, outreach, and instructional programs. It helps us assess how successful we are at generating awareness.

Dorm Surveys

Just as market researchers select specific towns or cities to test new approaches, librarians can similarly focus on student housing. This strategy is likely to provide you with a diverse, manageable population that can reveal generalized findings. Instead of relying on surveys that are self-selected or on completely random samples, you can hone in on a homogenous group of students living in close proximity. This gives you a chance to track word of mouth, peer influence, and shared experiences.

In order for this assessment to work you will most likely need the assistance of your campus housing office. I have found these staff members to be cooperative and generally willing to assist us with our academic mission. I recommend a short, one- or two-page, print survey that you can have resident assistants (RAs) distribute to each of their students. Although web-based surveys are more common, printed copies enable RAs to gather them quickly. By positioning the questionnaire with a function of dorm life, you will likely increase the response rate—and offering an incentive will increase responses even more.

Assessment at the dorm level provides an opportunity to collect some telling information. How many of the residents visited the library during the current semester? How frequently did they visit, and how long did they stay? How many of them checked out books or accessed an article online? How many of them went to the library with their fellow dorm mates? This type of data lets us gauge usage of library products at a very micro-level. We could also test recall and awareness of our promotional campaigns and word of mouth. Did they hear or see any information about events in the library? Did any of their professors bring up the library during class? Did they remember seeing the table tents we placed in the dining hall? We could provide them with a list of library services or resources and ask them to identify any that they have heard about or used. Along with all other forms of assessment, I suggest adding a chance for students to opt in for a follow-up questionnaire or focus group participation.

Longitudinal Study

While surveys, focus groups, usage statistics, and calls to action can help us evaluate our marketing programs, they provide a single snapshot of student life. One of the strongest, although time-consuming, efforts that we can make is an ongoing longitudinal study. This approach allows you to track student library usage over time, seeing precisely what products they use and how they discovered them. This type of study reveals academic life as it unfolds.

Each year I select six freshmen who stretch across different social segmentations. While this may not be scientific, it enables me to keep tabs on select user groups. My intention is not to push information out to them but, on the contrary, to pull experiences from them. I meet with each student once per semester and send a monthly e-mail that typically contains one or two broad questions (Have you ever used the library to study with a group?) as well as one or two specific to them (Has your library usage changed now that you are in your second year?).

What I am especially interested in is how they first find out about the library and what impressions they form during these initial experiences. I also extend this inquiry to find out how they approach assignments and when they start using the book collections, databases, software, and other more advanced services. Their responses provide a great way to test recall to see if they remember encountering any of our marketing messages. Additionally, I can detect if students notice changes that we make to spaces, policies, services, or equipment. A longitudinal group offers many advantages, particularly the chance to gather unbiased and unprompted information from select users. On a small scale we can discover areas where we succeed, fail, or miss out on opportunities to reach students.

DEFINING SUCCESS

When it comes to assessment there is no silver bullet. Just as there is no single best way to communicate with students, measuring the impact of advertising requires a triangulation of metrics. What it ultimately comes down to is how we define success. This is much clearer in business, where profits, sales, and new customers are reliable indicators of the direction in which a company is heading. What companies are after is a larger share of the consumer's wallet, but how does this translate for libraries? Our goals are multifaceted. Do we want a greater percentage of students visiting the library or people spending more time and using more services? Do we aim for greater familiarity or greater efficiency on the part of our users? And does it matter if students are satisfied, or are we more concerned about educating them on using the library properly?

I think that success, from a marketing standpoint, is a combination of familiarity along with usage, across the span of the student's tenure. The longevity of library use from day one until graduation is what matters. This should not be based on how many books we add to the collection or how many of them get checked out, but rather on how many different products students encounter and use.

Here is what I recommend. Take your inventory sheet from chapter 4 and list all the items that are relevant to undergraduates. Toward the end of the academic year, ask a random sample of thirty students from different classes (freshmen, sophomores, juniors, and seniors) to circle all the library products that they have heard of and, second, to place a checkmark beside all the ones that they have used. Once you have calculated these scores you can track both the effectiveness of your communication program, as well as the overall usage of the library. This method provides you with a sweeping overview of both awareness and utilization and presents a measurable goal in striving to increase both areas. Just as companies try to gain a larger share of their customers' wallets, we can try to encourage our users to take better advantage of all the services that we have to offer.

Success is subjective and can be difficult to pinpoint. I feel that instead of simply focusing on generating awareness or even just increasing use of resources, we should approach communication more philosophically by viewing our marketing as a chance to elevate the role of the library in our students' minds. In this manner, our advertising encourages them to expect more from us. We are not just providing more books, more journals, more computers, or more staff to help them, but rather more relevance. We should aspire to smash their preconceptions of what a library is and instead demonstrate what it can become.

NOTES

1. Rex Briggs and Greg Stuart, *What Sticks: Why Most Advertising Fails and How to Guarantee Yours Succeeds* (Chicago: Kaplan, 2006).
2. Brian Mathews and Jon Bodnar, *Promoting the Library, SPEC Kit 306* (Washington, DC: Association of Research Libraries, 2008).
3. Paul Farris and others, *Marketing Metrics: 50+ Metrics Every Executive Should Master* (Upper Saddle River, NJ: Wharton School, 2006); John Davis, *Measuring Marketing: 103 Key Metrics Every Marketer Needs* (Hoboken, NJ: Wiley, 2007).
4. Michael Whang, "Measuring the Success of the Academic Library Website Using Banner Advertisements and Web Conversation Rates: A Case Study," *Journal of Web Librarianship* 1 (2007): 93–108.
5. Mary Tyler and Jerri Ledford, *Google Analytics* (Indianapolis: Wiley, 2006).

11 Putting It All Together

The challenge in putting it all together is that every library is different. There are so many types of institutions: some are large research universities, while others are small liberal arts colleges; some cater to commuters, while others have a substantial on-campus population; some have one library, and others have several specialized branches; some have a large staff with highly focused positions, and others have a small staff where everyone does a little of everything. This multiplicity makes it difficult, if not impossible, to offer a model because what works in some libraries won't work at others.

Your organizational structure factors into this as well. Is it a hierarchical or a flat model? Does the administration control messaging, or do departments have free reign? The personality of your campus culture also plays a part in the tone and delivery channels that you should use. Some schools are bubbling with school spirit, while others are more apathetic. Some emphasize athletics, some the arts. Some have a large Greek system, and others have a majority of commuters or distance learners. Some are rural, some are urban, and some are online. Many schools also cater to a particular religion, gender, ethnic group, or discipline. All of these aspects that make our schools diverse will influence the way that we communicate with students. Try to absorb these unique traits and highlight them in your marketing efforts.

My goal in this book has been to stimulate your creative juices and help you think more intricately about reaching students. Our libraries have a lot to offer, and what it really comes down to is a matter of packaging our value in a way that makes sense and appeals to our community. In this final chapter, I offer several examples that incorporate all of the techniques described in this text, as well as a few lessons I've learned along the way.

Who's in charge? Every library approaches marketing a little differently. Most often it is either controlled at the administrative level or run by a committee. I have found that endeavors work best when a large group guides the general effort, but individuals have the freedom to develop projects on their own. In this way, the equivalent of the PR and marketing committee serves as a council, ensuring that everyone stays on message; yet subgroups take on specific ventures, bringing in other staff members when appropriate. Marketing works best when the people involved are passionate about the task, so let people take ownership for ideas that interest them.

Don't plan too much. I think it is a mistake to invest too much time on a formal marketing plan. Don't get me wrong: we definitely want some parameters to keep us moving in the right direction, but an elaborate marketing and communication plan will be outdated by the time you finish writing it. Don't let yourself be held back by assumptions you made a year or two ago. Another common problem that I have seen with library marketing plans is that they tend to be based on the organization's strategic plan. I fear that this approach focuses too much on promoting the library's own interests instead of meeting the needs of the user. Additionally, we risk spending too much time planning and not enough time actually interacting with our audience. I think that a better approach is to focus on three or four high-priority projects each semester, allowing some flexibility for opportunities that land in your lap. When you're starting out, it is valuable for the team to gain experience together. Academic years are very cyclical, so experiment with new ideas each semester and build on successes. In short, your time is limited; rather than spending months wordsmithing a mission statement or writing elaborate goals, develop short-term projects that will have a high impact and address the needs of diverse student segments.

Everyone participates in research. If you have a marketing committee, make sure that everyone is involved in the research process. You want everyone to be on the same page, so reviewing data, reading feedback, observing library usage, and hearing from students firsthand enables the team to form a shared understanding about the direction in which you should go.

Keep a cumulative list of promotional ideas. These might emerge from internal brainstorming, marketing research, or other libraries. Review your list every summer to see if a particular project fits into the upcoming year. Always keep expanding upon your ideas.

Generate a calendar of important dates. Include academic and social activities, such as orientations, popular sporting events, midterms, finals, and deadlines for major assignments. A calendar view allows you to monitor the student mindset and to identify ideal times for library programs. For example, homecoming week is probably not the best time for drop-in instruction sessions.

Grow your contacts. I highly recommend compiling a Rolodex of student ambassadors. Form a network of students who are passionate, sympathetic, or regular library service users. You need allies who can help you develop promotional material and spread positive word of mouth. Be sure to target different segments to ensure a wide reach of your message.

Get the message right first. In the beginning stages of developing a campaign, don't focus too much on the delivery method. It's easy to get sidetracked with *where* you are going to put your content instead of *what* you are going to say.

Start small. You can get overwhelmed by all the possibilities. Don't feel that you have to do everything all at once. Start by developing a few key projects that can reach a wide audience and then experiment with one or two specialized segments. This approach allows you to gauge what works and what doesn't and provides some team-building experience. When I started out it took me two full semesters to really understand the campus culture before I could conduct any large-scale campaigns.

Never again utter the words, "But we've always done it this way in the past."

Feedback should be ongoing. Talk with representatives of your target audience before, during, and after each campaign. Have them respond to your initial concepts to see if you are on the right track. Next, have them review your preliminary design: posters, fliers, web content, wording, or giveaways. And finally, talk with students after the campaign has run its course in order to measure the degree of success and gather ideas for the next time around. Including student feedback throughout development can save you from an embarrassing or futile result.

Follow the story. When developing a campaign, make sure that you fully understand the service or resource from the student's point of view. We might lose this perspective because we work closely with our products every day. I think it helps to envision students using the library by framing it as a story. What is the first experience like for freshmen? How do groups use the space to do their work? Also consider the sequence of actions: A student is writing a paper and needs to find a book. She struggles with the catalog and approaches the reference desk. A librarian helps her identify some titles. The student searches the stacks. Depending on how you read it, this could be a helpful or frustrating experience. By creating a visual narrative, your marketing team can address the questions, problems, uncertainties, and difficulties that users come upon. Don't pay attention only to what students are doing, but also to their moods, emotions, and motivations. Once you unlock those, your message becomes incredibly more effective.

Don't try to force round pegs into square holes. Some ideas just don't work, and you have to know when to cut your losses and move on. Maybe there is a project that worked well in the past or just *seems* like something the library should be doing, but if students don't respond, then there is probably another idea that will have more impact.

Have fun. Marketing should be fun. You get to be creative, interact with students, and work with staff on interesting projects. While our goal may be to promote the library, the big-picture idea is that we get to help students be successful. Remember, this is all really about them.

EXAMPLES

Here are four examples illustrating how all the pieces fit together to form a complete campaign message. More examples can be found on my blog at http://theubiquitouslibrarian.typepad.com.

EXAMPLE 1
Use the Library Every Day

Synopsis

This brand campaign will feature syndicated videos of students demonstrating how library services, spaces, and resources fit into their normal routines. Rather than being a place that students visit occasionally, this effort will place the library as a central hub on campus that students might visit regularly. Additionally, this promotion will show how the library evolves with student needs throughout the semester and over an extended period.

Background Research

Conduct three focus groups: one with second-term freshmen, one with sophomores and juniors, and one with seniors. Find out about their initial library interactions, with an emphasis on what services and resources they use, how they found out about them, and what they find confusing.

Administer a campuswide poll gauging the brand identity of the library. If the results uncover an image problem, it can be corrected; if the image is positive, then those features perceived as best should be highlighted.

Observe students using every product that the library offers; interview random users to gain insight into how and why they use particular items.

Brand Strategy

Image. "Meet me at the library," "A place for you," "There is something for everyone," or "The library: it's more than you think." Emphasize the wide spectrum of products and ways to use the library, from a comfortable lounge and relaxing coffee shop, to a more intense quiet study or group collaboration environment. Along with floors of books and scholarly journals, students can also discover entertainment and leisure materials, as well as workshops, events, fun activities, computers, and research assistance.

Value statement. The library is a suite of tools, services, and spaces carefully selected to fill a variety of student needs.

Emotional statement. You can always find what you need here. Build on the theme of the library being more than users might expect. It is a blend of intellectual, cultural, and social experiences, but also a place where they can turn for help or direction.

Product Inventory

This campaign strives to create a brand message—it is the overall concept of the library that is being presented. Therefore, the full product inventory should be considered, although emphasis should be given to the most practical services and resources, as well as ones that students commonly ask questions about.

Objectives

The primary objective is to expand the positive perception of the library. This campaign will challenge preconceptions that students may have and paint the library as being more than they might have anticipated.

Additionally, the effort will attempt to attract new users, expand the usage of current users, and highlight specific library products.

Target Audience

This campaign is intended to reach all members of the user community, with an emphasis on students living on campus.

Time Line

This campaign will run for the full academic year. The first half of the fall semester will feature casual library encounters, moving to more serious usage as the semester progresses. In this manner, the messaging evolves along with the students' needs and mindset. The promotion during the first half of the spring semester will serve to remind students about the library, with the "down to business" attitude emerging after spring break.

Building Blocks

The primary component of this campaign will be a series of videos that will air on the campus television station, be hosted on YouTube and iTunes U, and be embedded on a library website. A cast of three students, each one representing a different target segment, will highlight the library through their own varied usage. This campaign unfolds naturally as a narrative of their lives throughout the semester. The students selected are all friends of the library.

Cast

a freshman girl who discovers the library through novice eyes

a popular fraternity guy entering his final year, buckling down and starting to think more about life after college

a sophomore art student who is eccentric yet charismatic

The students will be given a digital camcorder, a digital camera, and a blog to chronicle their school year. The series will be framed like a reality TV show delivered in short weekly increments. Cast members will be encouraged to explore library products and other parts of campus, yet will have the freedom to post what they want. A librarian will work with them to develop possible content.

Suggested material: getting coffee; printing; scanning notes; meeting a friend; using reserves; resting between classes; using wireless; looking for books; searching for articles; meeting with a study group; practicing a presentation; getting help from a librarian, writing assistant, or teaching assistant; renting DVDs; borrowing equipment; using software; reading textbooks; coding web pages; and attending events. The overarching theme is to show all the different things that students can do in the library.

Posters and fliers in the library and around campus will be used to promote the series.

Message Attributes

Surprising. The surprise is in the subtlety of the campaign; it is like a reality TV show. This soft sell of the library will be unexpected and ideally will become an embedded part of campus culture that is both entertaining and educational.

Relatable. Students are the face of this campaign, demonstrating to their peers the many uses of the library. The product highlights will be directly tied to particular needs or course work.

Tangible. Videos will be collected on YouTube, where they will be tangible in a virtual sense; however, fliers promoting the campaign URL will also be distributed in high-traffic areas on campus.

Experiential. The experience is derived from anticipating the next video or promotional pieces. Similar to watching a television show or other syndicated content, the audience awaits the next installment. Another layer of the experience emerges when students actually use the services that the so-called stars use; for example, when they come into the library with the intention of scanning or when they access articles through a featured database. From an advertising perspective, the series website will allow students to submit their own library stories, photos, video, research tips, and suggestions for improvement.

Shareable. Most of the content is digital, making it easy for students to share with others. The real test is how well students connect with the material; is it something that they want to pass along to others, something they talk about? The star power of the students involved will influence the popularity.

Measurable. The website and video hit counts will be used to keep track of visitors to gauge popularity. Additionally, comments and message board posts will indicate attention from the audience. Campuswide polls could be conducted occasionally to measure student awareness of the programming. Any questions or feedback that the cast receives can also be evaluated. Indirectly, a rise in the usage of services that they mention might be attributed to the campaign.

EXAMPLE 2
Multimedia Contest

Synopsis

A multimedia contest will serve as a means for promoting a variety of library products. Entries can be submitted for video, animation, or graphical design categories. Through library efforts in advertising the competition, students will gain awareness of numerous resources and services of which they were likely unaware that the library provided. The winners of the contest will be announced at a library-sponsored award show where the creative works of the students will be displayed.

Background Research

Interview library student assistants and staff in the multimedia center about support and recommendations for the contest.

Interview several graphic and multimedia design majors and faculty members about potential interest, feasibility, and recommendations. Also gather their opinions on the best way to advertise the contest.

Review usage statistics of related library resources, such as Safari Tech Books, multimedia equipment circulation, Mac log-ins, and assistance inquiries.

Brand Strategy

Image. "Show us your stuff!" "Make something cool!" Students should be challenged. Inspire their creativity. More than a library contest, this is rather a campuswide competition and their chance to show off their talent.

Value statement. The library offers a wide range of multimedia-related products and services. Students can develop skills that would also be useful for personal and class projects.

Emotional statement. Dreams are designed here. The library is a place for the imagination and creative output.

Product Inventory

The multimedia studio

Resources: Safari Tech Books, e-book collection, print book collection, DVDs, and online tutorials

Software: Flash, Photoshop, film and audio editing, and other multimedia programs

Equipment: digital cameras, video recorders, audio recorders, laptops, Wacom tablets, webcams, microphones, and other gadgets

Assistance: reference desk and multimedia student assistants

Objectives

To promote awareness and the use of the multimedia studio and related resources

To promote attendance at the awards show event

To increase the positive perception of the library as modern and technology-rich

To engage the campus community in a creative contest

Target Audience

The contest is open to all students.

The library will target the artistic segment by appealing to majors, courses, and student groups associated with art, design, computer science, creative writing, and multimedia.

Time Line

Weeks 3–5: General information announcing the contest

Weeks 6–8: Specialized information about the contest; mention award shows

Week 9: The last call for submissions; big push for the award show

Week 10: Continued promotion for the awards show at the end of the week

Building Blocks

A contest website will provide details, rules, and criteria. The page will also provide information about equipment, training, software, assistance, and other associated library products. Additionally, a message board and contact e-mail address will also be available.

Include information on the campus and library calendars; add banner ads to the library home page rotation and library news blog.

Colorful and energetic posters will be displayed in the library, student center, dorms, classrooms, bus stops, and other computer labs on campus. During the initial two weeks, make as big a splash as possible.

Develop advertising for the campus television station, campus radio, and campus newspaper.

Send out a press release to the campus newspaper.

E-mail professors about the contest and encourage them to pass along information to their students.

Multimedia studio staff will create two Flash animation commercials: one promoting the contest and the other promoting the awards show.

Offer multimedia training classes and workshops.

Host a social event for students interested in the contest. Provide free snacks and the opportunity for them to learn more about the multimedia studio and to interact with each other. This could lead to a collaborative group submission effort.

Give away T-shirts designed to promote the contest.

Create a Facebook group and buy targeted ads.

Highlight guest judges.

Each day during the week leading up to the awards show, feature a different submitted video, animation, or graphic file on the library home page to generate interest.

Host an awards show to screen the best entries and to reward the winners with great prizes.

Message Attributes

Surprising. A multimedia contest by its very nature is surprising for an academic library. Undergraduates don't traditionally associate a creative competition with libraries. Even if a student has no interest in participating, he may still find out about all of the various products connected to the contest.

Relatable. Multimedia is a regular component of the Millennials' culture. Likewise, many courses now require students to develop a supplemental artifact, such as a video or website. This contest appeals to both the entertainment as well as scholarly needs of students.

Tangible. A cool flier is necessary in order to catch students' eyes. This contest will be very visible on campus, so providing a flier that directs them to the contest website will encourage them to find out more. Additionally, explore giveaways like T-shirts, stickers, or something unusual such as an origami promotional piece.

Experiential. The contest encourages students to create a piece of multimedia, and, therefore, the experience occurs through participation. Resulting student actions could be attending a class, reviewing a tutorial, reading an e-book, or using another library service in some manner. From a promotional standpoint, the website should include interactive content, such as a message board or blog for students to post questions or submit ideas, as well as a video highlighting library resources.

Shareable. Make information about the contest easy for others to pass along to their friends who may have artistic skills. Group entries will be allowed, building on a collaborative design. When promoting the awards show, release a few of the best or most unusual entries early, in the hope that students will share them with friends.

Measurable. Use Google Analytics on the contest website to monitor traffic and to determine how visitors found the site. Submissions, inquiries, message board activity, and awards show attendance will factor into the assessment. Increased usage statistics for multimedia equipment, software, e-resources, training materials, and assistance can also be used to determine the impact of the contest. Additionally, conduct biweekly campuswide polls in order to gauge awareness and interest in the contest and the awards show.

EXAMPLE 3
Promoting a Database

Synopsis

The goal of this campaign is to promote library resources to biology majors. The focus will center on BIOSIS, a comprehensive database for the life sciences. The effort will also emphasize related services and resources. Instead of simply trying to push the database, the approach will show how library tools are used in the profession and attempt to create a sense of curiosity about performing research.

Background Research

Review usage statistics for BIOSIS and the biology subject guide.

Interview biology faculty on how they conduct research and the types of course work they assign to students.

Generate a list of biology courses that involve a research component.

Facilitate two focus groups with biology students. Explore their current research practices, views on the curriculum, previous library experience, and reasons for choosing to study biology.

Poll biology majors to gauge their initial familiarity with BIOSIS.

Brand Strategy

Image. "BIOSIS is biology" or "Biologists use BIOSIS." Associate the discipline with the database—it is Google for biologists.

Value statement. BIOSIS is not just a website for finding articles, but it is also a professional tool for locating scientific research.

Professionals turn to this database when they need to find answers, and now students have access to its body of information.

Emotional statement. Build on the idea that anyone can use Google or the open Web, but BIOSIS is an elite product, designed specifically for biology majors, researchers, faculty, and doctors. It also collects the types of materials that professors want their students to use.

Product Inventory

BIOSIS and other biology-related databases

Supplemental services: reference assistance, biology subject guide, library events, monograph and journal collections, tutorials, and event spaces

Objectives

To increase the awareness and usage of BIOSIS

To increase overall usage and positive perception of the library

Target Audience

All members of the campus's biology community

Time Line

Fall semester, weeks 3–12

Building Blocks

A website will serve as the central portal for the campaign; all other promotional material will direct users to the URL. The site will feature basic information about BIOSIS and other tools, tutorials, testimonials, a calendar, a message board, a link to the biology subject guide, and the contact information for the life sciences librarian.

Posters in the biology building will direct students to the URL. These items will feature personalities from the field (faculty, researchers, Nobel Prize winners, and other interesting doctors or scientists), as well as medical and scientific breakthroughs and emerging technologies. This information could also be distilled into a flier or handout and distributed during class.

Posters will also be hung in the library stacks near appropriate LC ranges.

Coordinate events of interest to the biology community, such as tours of labs, field trips, guest lectures, biology club meetings, and discipline-specific social activities.

Plan two instructional sessions that will bring together the life sciences subject librarian with teaching assistants and writing center staff.

Message Attributes

Surprising. Instead of relying on the authority of BIOSIS, the campaign will appeal to the user's sense of curiosity. Build around the idea of the *biology community* to pique interest and incite the desire for belonging.

Relatable. Demonstrate how library products match student needs. BIOSIS is a tool that all biology majors use. Promotions should highlight images, stories, and motivations that emerged during initial focus groups.

Tangible. Fliers announcing the various events should be distributed to the target audience. Consider T-shirts or related giveaways. Check with BIOSIS and the School of Biology for freebies.

Experiential. On an abstract level, the experience occurs when the student starts using BIOSIS and, hence, officially buys into the idea of the community. In a more direct way, the experience comes from interacting with faculty and students and learning more about their major.

Shareable. The campaign should be designed with word of mouth in mind. Biology students will discuss the events, promotional material, and resources as part of their natural conversations.

Measurable. Several methods can be used for assessment: website hits; number of tutorial views; BIOSIS statistics; attendance at events; and a post-campaign survey, focus group, and poll.

EXAMPLE 4
"How Many Books Can You Check Out?"

Note: This campaign works best if users are allowed to check out a large number of books—at least fifty. In my library there is no limit, which surprises and delights students.

Synopsis

This campaign emphasizes the large number of books that users are permitted to borrow. The slogan can be read in two ways: (1) as a challenge encouraging students to check out as many books as they can and (2) as a question inquiring as to the limit of books that students can have out at one time. Each month a new user will be highlighted on posters showing the enormous number of monographs they have borrowed.

Background Research

Poll students early in the semester to find out how many books they believe they can check out.

Review circulation statistics: total volumes checked out per semester and total number of unique users who have borrowed books per semester.

Brand Strategy

Image. "How many books can you check out?" Photos will include students and faculty with enormous amounts of library books. The impression should be humorous and awe-inspiring.

Value statement. The library has a massive amount of books on a wide range of subjects. Comparably it would require twenty Barnes & Noble bookstores to match the number of volumes offered by the library.

Emotional statement. The library has your information needs covered.

Product Inventory

The large collection and variety of books. Other items that may surface include e-books, journals, CDs, and DVDs.

Services that could potentially emerge in supplemental material: interlibrary loan, holds, and recalls.

Objectives

The primary objective of this campaign is to promote awareness and increase usage of library collections.

The campaign will also attempt to positively expand user perceptions of the library.

Target Audience

All members of the campus community.

There may be some extra emphasis on freshman dorms.

Time Line

This will be an ongoing campaign, with new posters developed monthly during the fall and spring semesters.

Building Blocks

Posters of book-borrower honorees will be prominently displayed in the library and on campus. These will feature eye-catching images, such as a dorm room filled to the ceiling with books, a student lugging a wheelbarrow of books around, or a professor with piles of books in his office. These posters should be good-natured and funny. Besides sheer volume, the poster could also emphasize strengths of the collection such as business books or sci-fi titles.

Short video clips featuring the borrowers may be developed to serve as a testimonial of the library collection. These could be spotlighted periodically on the library home page.

A website collecting photos, stories, videos, and recommendations of these prolific library users will be developed.

Message Attributes

Surprising. The images should be astonishing. Students are probably aware that the library has a large collection, but seeing someone with fifty or one hundred books puts it in perspective. The library might also post the total number of books checked out each week to drive home the volume of activity. Additionally, each poster could be supplemented by a publicity stunt, such as someone actually pushing a wheelbarrow of books around campus or student-athletes stacking books in their hands to see how many they can carry.

Relatable. Most students may not check out an enormous number of books, but the campaign serves as a reminder about the campus library. The relevant theme is that students can turn to the library when they need scholarly material.

Tangible. Give away a limited number of tote bags with the "How many books can you check out?" slogan. Wacky stickers may be given out to students reaching certain benchmarks, such as fifty, one hundred, or five hundred books.

Experiential. Students will be encouraged to ask for their total cumulative book count at the circulation desk. The campaign website will also feature instructional content, library floor plans, a link to new titles added to the collection, and a book recommendation form.

Shareable. This campaign may create word of mouth. With humorous posters, videos, and publicity stunts set at monthly intervals, students will likely talk about library collections with their friends.

Measurable. Poll students during the middle and end of the semester to see if they know how many books they can check out. Review circulation statistics to see if the total book count and number of unique borrowers have increased. Monitor web traffic to the related website. Review longitudinal LibQUAL+ data to see if perceptions of the collection have improved.

Epilogue

Staging Academic Experiences

I LEARNED A LOT ALONG THE JOURNEY of writing this book. The main takeaway: we can never do enough marketing. Every outreach attempt that we make has some degree of positive impact but doesn't reach everyone. Students discover the library differently, and we need to be conscious of that in the way that we present it to them. I've asked many students point-blank, what's the best way for the library to share information with you, and their responses reveal a gaping contrast. Some encourage us to send them e-mails, while others admit they would never read them. Some suggest putting information on our website, on posters, or on fliers, while others explained that they ignored these channels. Some thought that faculty could do more to promote the library, while others claimed they would only listen to professors if it were related to an assignment.

Just as people have different learning styles and study preferences, they also absorb communications differently. What works well for some doesn't necessarily work for others, and so if our goal is to reach as many students as possible, then we need to diversify the ways to deliver our message. What I have found is that there isn't necessarily any one approach or one particular communication channel that works best, but rather it is the combined effort of all of them working together that makes promotions successful. The more exposure we can gain, the better off we are. By getting students talking about the library, using our services, searching our databases, and working on assignments in our spaces, then the *idea* of the library will spread. I don't see our goal being to simply draw students in, but rather to draw them together. By appealing to their sense of community and giving them a way to belong, the library becomes an even more essential player on campus.

Addressing a wider variety of student needs is critical for future-thinking libraries. In many respects, this change movement is already under way. The rapid adoption of the commons model pulls together tools, technology, people, and collaborative spaces. Although we use many different names—learning commons, information commons, study commons, or intellectual commons—the goal is essentially the same. We are updating the library in order to accommodate a changing curriculum. Now a student can not only access material and get help, but also download and configure data, create graphics, edit a video clip, design a website, and write a paper, all from one spot.

Libraries are not changing just because they can, but rather because they have to. It isn't Google or the Web that makes us outdated; it is an assortment of new skill sets and assignments that are required of our students. Not only do they find and access information in new ways, but they are using and presenting this material differently as well. A common desire that we have is to bring the library into the classroom. This mindset typically centers around instructing students on how to use library resources and helping them become better researchers; however, a more advantageous approach would be to focus instead on helping them become better communicators.

This model offers an interactive approach to assignments; not only are students conducting research and composing a paper, but they are involved in creating an artifact and presenting what they have learned as well. (See figure E.1.) Libraries are perfectly positioned to promote this modern application of scholarship, which encourages students to discover, design, and display information. Instead of just writing, students develop, describe, and demonstrate their ideas. This transforms an assignment into an academic experience, allowing students not only to investigate a topic, but to further immerse themselves in the process.

This evolutionary path for the academic library pushes us into a more dynamic role as facilitators of communication, rather than mere collectors of information. The media-rich library prepares students for the professional workplace, not just for writing term papers. In this way, the library provides exposure to interdisciplinary content, emerging technologies, and multiple forms of expression, as well as to critical thinking and analytical skills.

Here's how it might work: each class will take on a broad topic, such as homelessness, environmentalism, immigration, alternative energy,

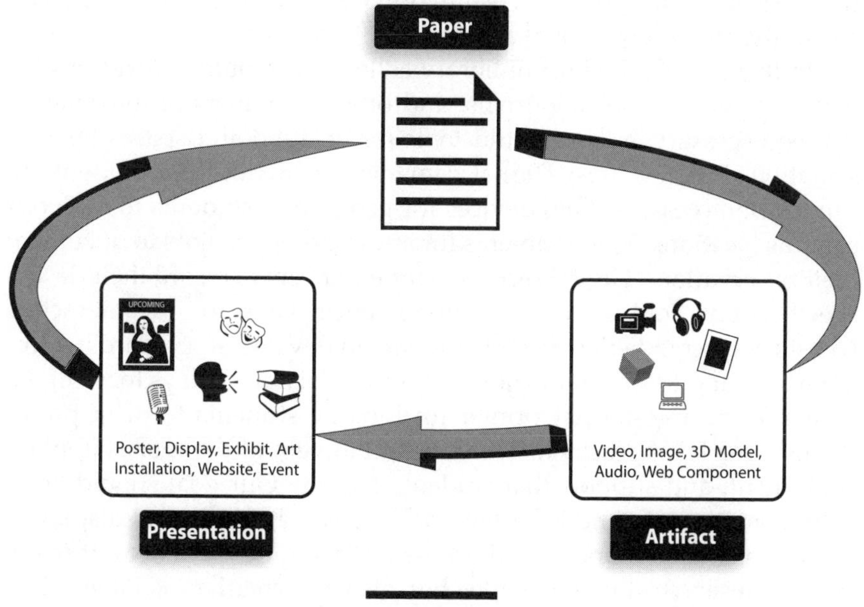

FIGURE E.1
Active-learning assignment circle

health care, or globalization. Students will independently explore a different strand or angle of the topic and conduct research in the traditional manner. Class discussions throughout this process will reinforce what they are learning, with each person contributing to the overall knowledge of the topic. Students will also work together to gather original material through observations, interviews, surveys, fieldwork, or other methods. Groups will develop their findings into a written report and also design a supporting artifact. This supplementary material could be a map, a 3-D model, a poster, a web tool—something interactive that accompanies their research. Students will also present their work, not just to each other, but beyond the classroom. A project fair could be hosted in the library or somewhere else on campus, or even at a community center or other appropriate location off campus. This gives the students a chance to showcase their work, present their ideas, and dialogue with outsiders. Displays could be a traditional lecture or presentation, or poster sessions, exhibits, websites, videos, digital objectives, or panel discussions. All of these components come together to make scholarship an experiential enterprise, enabling students to become proficient with reasoning and research, teamwork, leadership, time management, creativity, and interpersonal and presentation skills.

In this regard, the idea of library collections would expand greatly. Not only would books, journals, and other containers of information still be necessary, but so would tools for creation and spaces for presentation. Imagine this: Digital cameras for architecture students to use for photo essays. GPS devices for geography students to map our campus locations. Video cameras for anthropology majors to document their observations. Digital recorders for engineers to record their design specifications. Software for computer science majors to code interactive websites. Wacom tablets for art students to develop storyboards. Acres of virtual land for theater majors to interpret classical plays for a digital audience. A large-format printer for biology students to print poster sessions for DNA research. Think imaginatively of the tools, supplies, equipment, and support that students require. Our goal should be to help them not only find information, but create it, use it, and display it.

The academic library can become a place for experiences. It is not just for research and reflection, but also for creation, collaboration, design, and exhibition. The library functions as a workshop, a gallery, a museum, a canvas, a stage, a lecture hall, a platform, a case study, and a showcase of student work. The future of libraries isn't simply about digitizing all of our collections, but rather it is about providing, encouraging, and staging new types of learning encounters. Instead of using marketing to try to persuade students to use our services, the library becomes the natural setting for academic activities—an environment where scholarship happens.

Afterword

ON MANY CAMPUSES THE LIBRARY IS JUST a place where dust collects on top of books for the majority of the term. Toward the end of the semester it explodes—bursting at the seams with students who don't know where things are or how to use the resources provided for them. Ultimately there's an exodus, and students go back to their social lives in niches across campus.

At Georgia Tech, our library is different. Its tables are packed with students from the first week of the semester, with study groups and social events. Our library isn't just a place where people come to find a quiet corner. We meet with friends between classes to grab a sandwich and a smoothie. We make time at night to convene to exchange notes and gossip. People lament when the doors are closed each Friday evening and revolt when things are changed without notice. It's because of our attitude, and the library staff's willingness to accept it, that we've developed such a community around a single building on campus.

The library is our home away from home—a place to eat, sleep, study, and socialize. It's our anchor during our busiest weeks—a place to relax while still in a learning environment. It's our solace in the midst of finals—a place to read a book or cruise the Web. The library is our campus commune.

Amanda McNamee
Student at the Georgia
Institute of Technology

Afterword

Index

You may also be interested in

Creating the Customer-Driven Academic Library: With more and more scholarly content available online and accessible almost anywhere, where does the traditional "brick and mortar" library fit in? In this book Jeannette Woodward confronts this and other pressing issues facing today's academic librarians. Her trailblazing strategies center on keeping the customer's point of view in focus at all times to help you keep customers coming through the door.

The Academic Library and the Net Gen Student: As students embrace new Web 2.0 technologies like MySpace, YouTube, and RSS feeds, libraries also need to take charge. This book will help academic librarians in public services, technology, and administration to better understand the integral role of technology in the social and academic lives of undergraduates, the Net Generation.

Transforming Library Service through Information Commons: This invaluable guide provides the "how-to" information necessary for institutions considering the development of an information commons. Offering plain-speaking advice on what works, authors Bailey and Tierney provide comprehensive case studies from small and large academic libraries to help librarians implement, provide training for, market, and assess an information commons.

Protecting Intellectual Freedom in Your Academic Library: This book, tailored to the academic library environment, presents a number of scenarios in which intellectual freedom is at risk. It includes case studies that provide narrative treatment of common situations, easy and motivating ways to prepare new hires for handling intellectual freedom issues, sidebars throughout the book that offer sample policies, definitions of key terms, and analysis of important statutes and decisions, and detailed information on how to handle challenges to materials in your collection.

Check out these and other great titles at www.alastore.ala.org!